I'M
NOT
F*CKING
ANGRY!

I'M
NOT
F*CKING
ANGRY!

ADJUST THE FLAME
TO GET WHAT YOU
WANT AND NEED

DR. MITCH ABRAMS

MUNN
AVENUE
PRESS

I'M NOT F*CKING ANGRY!

Adjust the Flame to Get What You Want and Need
by Dr. Mitch Abrams

First Edition
Copyright © 2025 by Dr. Mitch Abrams

Published by
Munn Avenue Press
300 Main Street, Ste 21
Madison, NJ 07940
MunnAvenuePress.com

Paperback ISBN: 978-1-969679-00-1
Hardcover ISBN: 978-1-969679-01-8
Audiobook ISBN: 978-1-969679-06-3
Printed in the United States of America

For my mother, who advised me: "Get that shit under control (my anger), or it's going to ruin your life..."

CONTENTS

INTRODUCTION

"I'm NOT Fucking Angry!!"

How many times have you thought or said this, or even screamed it?

Do you ever feel ashamed to admit any other emotion besides anger? What is it about anger, and being angry, that unglues us so completely? With the exception of shame itself, there's no feeling we're more ashamed or embarrassed to admit than anger. But why?

These questions are part of a bigger issue. Many of us have a degree of alexithymia (a fancy word for being unable to label our emotions or identify other people's feelings), which is epidemic in our lives. Our modern world has only made this more pronounced, as we're constantly assaulted with information and our senses. We are fried and exhausted, struggling to keep up and understand. There's too much to take in and very little time to process any of it.

Think about the last time you received a text from someone and thought, *Huh?* Or more accurately, *What the fuck?!* You're left trying to read between the lines and searching for the tone or emotional inflection that will help you know what they meant, and how to respond. We can barely identify how *we* feel, never mind what someone else is trying to communicate. No wonder we're all stretched a bit thin. And what happens when we're overwhelmed? We lose it, act out, get super pissed off at things that usually don't matter, and take everything intensely and very personally. We overreact.

A lot of people have a hard time communicating in person, but by text, the way most communication works these days? That's an altogether different challenge. When you add the fact that so many people can't really identify how they feel or how other people feel, miscommunication—and hurt feelings, confusion, frustration, irritation, and, yes, anger—often follows.

In a world in which we communicate by short, often nonsensical incomplete thoughts and emojis, we think we're actually communicating, but we're not. We're barely scratching the surface. We use tiny cartoonish symbols to convey big human feelings, which for adults is silly and kind of embarrassing. What could go wrong? Turns out, nearly everything. We've taken alexithymia and turned it into a language that actually means nothing. So if someone sends you a text that reads, *I'm not fucking angry!*, I assure you, they are. You know it and so do they.

* * *

How the hell is someone going to *manage* how they feel if they can't even *identify* how they feel, and can't communicate these feelings in a productive way? After being an expert in anger management for over 25 years, working with prison inmates, professional athletes, CEOs, surgeons, housewives, and pretty much everyone under the sun with anger problems—and even for those for whom anger wouldn't be described as a "problem"—I am 100 percent confident that part of the issue is that no one has ever really communicated to us that it's okay to be angry, and it's totally normal to call it what it is. And not only is it okay, it's part of being human.

This book is going to dispel the myth that anger is a problem, and that angry people are always scary, bad, or dangerous. Nobody gets in trouble for *being* angry. People sometimes get in trouble for the stupid shit they *do* when they're angry, which is the difference between our thoughts, feelings, and actions. There's a monumental difference between our emotions and our behavior, and we're going to examine that difference. We'll also explore how you can take charge of your thoughts and feelings so they don't lead to behaviors that ruin your life. It's actually that simple: Anger can and *does* destroy otherwise functional and stable lives. But it doesn't have to, and all of the drama and chaos and destruction can be avoided.

Anger isn't really the problem we think it is, but the violence—both physical and emotional—it often leads to absolutely is. We've become alarmingly desensitized to violence in American society, so much so that we have to define what is *not* violence, versus what is. Mean words are not really violence. Someone being a dick is also not violence. Not getting what we want, when and how we want it, isn't violent, and being treated badly isn't the violence it feels like to us. However, how we react often is violent, and that's where the problem and destructive harm arise for so many of us.

So, since anger can be so harmful to our lives, why does it sometimes feel so good? It does two things: first, it sends a surge of adrenaline through our bodies. We get ready to fight, and it gives us all kinds of physiological signals to run, or do battle with whatever has pissed us off. In these moments, anger becomes a vehicle of our power. Whether we admit it or not, we long for being this powerful person, the one who isn't victimized, the one who calls the shots and is *effective*.

Effectiveness makes us feel strong, which is a feeling like no other.

But only sometimes, and most of us, when we feel this way, can't control or channel the anger. It delivers this brief chemical high that's intoxicating, reinforcing a feeling that we're actually in charge. We can dominate our environment, and some of the people in it, which strengthens our sense of self through dominance. Let's be honest with ourselves: Dominance can reward us for that behavior. It can feel amazing to be powerful and in charge. We want to feel like we're in total command of ourselves, masters of our domain, and not to be fucked with.

Anger can deliver these positive feelings, filling us with energy and focus, pumping us up, motivating us to act, and tricking us into thinking we can do anything. But that's the problem. Anger feels good because when our blood is saturated with adrenaline, we end up with a lot of tension in search of a release. And simply put: that's how people destroy their lives with anger. They unload in the wrong way, on the wrong people, at the wrong times, and in out-of-control ways.

I'd like to warn you—this book, though based on sound science and decades of my experience as a psychologist, isn't a research treatise. You're not going to hear my voice pontificating with an Ivy League, uptight, or judgmental tone. Instead, you'll hear my real voice, my Brooklyn accent, which is the place where anger seems to have been born, anyway.

Also: I'm not coming to this area of psychology from a politically correct point of view, but rather from a deeply informed and practical perspective. Some people will read this and think, *Damn, that's harsh, Doc.* That's okay with me, because anger is my area of expertise, and it's time we were more honest about what it is and how it works. Concealing it as a dirty secret isn't helping. Burying the truth about anger doesn't make it go away.

I'm exceptionally pragmatic and direct, and so is this book. This is the kind of honesty I use in my practice with people from all walks of life who are working to understand themselves better. Hopefully, you'll find it funny at times and feel more empowered as you navigate the relationships in your life, including the one with yourself."

Lastly, I'm not sorry for the profanity you'll see here. It's not added gratuitously; rather, reality dictates that when talking about extreme emotions, all language should be on the table. If you dropped an anvil on your foot, you wouldn't smile and say, "Spring is here!" You'd say, "Holy shit! I just broke my fucking foot!" If you're particularly offended by foul language, you probably want to put this book down. But don't think I don't know that you swear when you get pissed off, because most of us do.

Profanity is actually a really powerful tool, as the fluent swearers here know. It's pragmatic, direct, and extremely expressive, and from a cognitive, psychological angle, swearing communicates more emotion than the PG language we use. It requires creativity, can be extremely funny, and, believe it or not, these delicious, expressive words convey deeply emotionally arousing stimuli, to both the profane user and the listener. They connect us. Think of the most extreme potty mouth you know. Chances are, you're smiling and admiring how their well-placed f-bombs (or take your pick of words) landed a sentence you still remember, like verbal punctuation. These words are part of our language, and they're here to be used. Can they be insulting? Sure. We may want them to be. That's life. Sometimes, we want to assert ourselves by insulting someone. Hopefully not that often, but we all know it's going to happen from time to time.

While we're talking about language, I'll try to provide a new set of definitions and terminology, so we have a more pragmatic understanding of the differences between emotions and behavior, and so we can speak about these things in practical terms. Understanding anger from a broad perspective requires us to do something that's hard for anyone—taking a long, hard look at ourselves. *Really* looking, like we're meeting ourselves for the first time. It's not the easiest thing to do, but it works. Why? Because it allows us to see how and where anger has impacted us—both other people's lives and our own.

This kind of hard look is what I'm hopeful will be easier for you after you read this book. I hope you begin to see yourself with empathy and compassion—as someone you genuinely want to support in becoming better at life. I hope you realize that sometimes, you really are fucking angry, and there's nothing wrong with it, that it's part of the process.

1

YOU **ARE** FUCKING ANGRY (BUT IT'S TOTALLY NORMAL)

People often tell me, "I'm not angry," though I know they are, and what I'm hearing is that they just don't have the language to label their feelings. They may say that they're not angry because they think nobody's going to give a shit. No one's going to relate. They're alone in their emotions and can't communicate them to anyone who they think will actually really hear them and understand them. The truth is, *most* people are going to relate. Most people are going to understand, but that isn't going to excuse someone who's acting like an asshole.

How people label their emotions—or fail to—is a "multiply determined problem," which just refers to a situation where a particular outcome or behavior isn't caused by a single factor, but instead is the total of multiple variables or contributing elements. It would be normal to be angry when a half dozen things go wrong in succession, leaving a person feeling shitty and powerless, which is a common condition in a world in which things large and small go wrong all the time.

Labeling the emotions caused by a world filled with friction is a skill that you're either directly taught by your parents and your social experiences or you aren't. And if you don't know how you feel, you're going to be at a real disadvantage. So if you've never learned this skill, let's teach it to you now. Because if you can't, if you can't *identify* how you feel, how can you ever *manage* how you feel?

Since there's no such thing as a "bad" emotion, you can't fix a problem you can't acknowledge is there in the first place. Anger is like walking around with your emotional baggage right in front of you. Everyone else can see it, but you're the last person to know it's there. So, now is the time to take stock of your own personal anger load.

When I see someone carrying this weight of anger, I see someone who is often perceived as hostile. They may be waking up on the wrong side of the bed every day, and this becomes self-perpetuating because they become a miserable fuck who no one wants to talk to, relate to, or have to deal with. They become someone people try to avoid. Naturally, a person then gets sad about this, and that makes them angry too. People with serious anger problems get labeled as socially radioactive, primitive, savage beasts, when I think they're being tremendously misunderstood.

Anger is something we have at birth, before we've had any time to get pissed off about canceled flights, layoffs, cheating spouses, or any other of life's enraging experiences. Anger is a basic, fundamental thing hardwired in our DNA and our physiology. It is primitive, though we expect sophisticated, evolved, and civilized society to silence anger in us, making us all well-mannered and frictionless. But anger strips us of the refinement, self-control, and dignity we want to wear as our non-savage armor, since it makes us seem completely undignified.

The reason we come with an anger program fully loaded in our human operating system is because it helps us to survive. Anger helped our ancestors find the strength to take on a massive animal for food, because no one knew when their sorry ass was going to find another meal. Since surviving on berries wasn't working, some anger, at a moderate level, made us faster and stronger. It increased our stamina and decreased our perception of pain. Some anger helped our species survive because it enabled millennia of our ancestors to hunt, and being hungry and *just* angry enough helped us get our basic needs met.

In our sophisticated society, there's nothing more motivating than hearing "You can't do that" or "You're not capable of that." It inspires a cellular-level "Fuck you—watch me!" from most people. And by the way, I don't think any singular bit of self-talk fueled more people to success than "Fuck you—watch me!" Why? Because the opposite of aggressive is passive, and being completely passive means just waiting and hoping things come your way. But guess what? They don't. You have to reach for the things you want, and like our ancestors, the delicious mastodon wasn't going to walk into the cave and offer to roast itself.

To a degree, being aggressive is good, but people often confuse anger and aggression. When you're angry, you're aggressive, which is to be expected. But the truth is, "reactive aggression" is the problem, in which anger increases and gets out of control. In the right amount, anger helps us motivate ourselves to achieve what someone—or life— has told us we can't have. Then, it was food and shelter. Today, it's nearly everything in our complicated world. But no matter what era of history we look at, anger is an integral part of human survival.

The point is: If we're trying to become better versions of ourselves, some self-examination is required. But self-examination is really hard to do if you don't have self-awareness of your emotions. If you're so angry at the world because you've been served a shit sandwich, you can't accurately reflect on what's really going on in and around you. You're always going to be fighting the wrong fights and losing most of them.

Anger is an obstacle for many people, and it prevents them from having what they really want, which is actually within their reach more often than not. My experience confirms that anger is the fuel in our engines, taking us where we want to go. But for many people, it becomes the problem—the emotion they can't control—that makes things impossible for them. The world isn't doing this to us; we are doing it to ourselves. It's so simple, it's almost anticlimactic.

So what's the solution that helps us get out of our own way? When the stresses of life are weighing you down, will you let them destroy you? If you can imagine standing in a tank of water, like the one below, and there is a plexiglass ceiling that represents the hardships in life coming down on you, will you let it drown you? Or, will you brace your feet on the floor and throw it the fuck off? Learning to identify and harness your anger can make you unstoppable.

Life Stressors

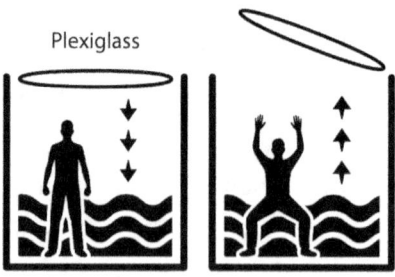

As the plexiglass, holding all of your life stressors weighing it down, comes down on you. As it lowers, it is now right above you. Eventually, it is pushing you under the water.

Will you submit and drown or brace your feet on the ground and throw the glass off of you?

I'd like to tell you a little about me, and what qualifies me to know what it means to say "I'm not fucking angry." I know a few things about anger. In fact, I'm an expert. Not only an expert at being angry, or having been, but an expert at treating anger. I know what happens when the only treatment occurs behind bars, and how much anger can spill out and destroy things. I've treated tens of thousands of people, helping them to harness what pisses them off, including thousands of athletes (at all levels) and even more incarcerated people. When I work with my clients, regardless of where they are in life or how they got there, something important emerges: They learn that they need to deal with their anger and channel it into something really helpful for them, or else it is going to deal with them. This sounds like an oversimplification, but it isn't.

Think about it this way: There isn't really a more extreme spectrum of opportunity than the differences between a professional athlete and a prisoner. One holds the world in their hands, earns a huge living, and is worshipped by fans. The other is so controlled, their every move is dictated by the criminal justice system. And yet, anger connects them. Athletes can harness their anger to achieve remarkable things: winning on the world's stage and earning the adulation of millions of people. And at the other extreme, it's often anger that landed my incarcerated clients behind bars. It's this extreme that led me to realize that the same mechanism that inspires an athlete on the court to channel their desire to a winning championship is what prevents someone in jail from controlling themselves enough to stay out of the system's crosshairs.

And this connection includes me, and my own experience with anger, which led me to where I am today. As a psychologist, I've had a lot of opportunities to think about how we end up where we do, and in my life, things could have gone either way. I write to you from a position of stability, authority, as much education as was possible, and knowledge, but I could also have been someone who ended up behind bars. It really could have gone either way for me. Learning to control what was boiling inside probably saved me and allowed me to create not only a productive life but also to keep my freedom.

* * *

I have a very intimate relationship with anger, and I don't really remember a time when I didn't feel it. I grew up in one of the poorest families in a poor neighborhood, in a part of Brooklyn that tourists don't visit for artisanal coffee and overpriced, destination donuts. I was angry about all of the things that the other kids had that my parents couldn't afford. I learned how to recognize and master my anger, and it led to my work in several different places throughout my education, which taught me about anger management.

Whether it was navigating bullies at school (I was far more likely to take them on and protect the underdog) or being a slowly assimilated outcast as I went to high school in a less diverse demographic than I lived in through middle school, the "kid from the streets" attitude that I grew up with in Starrett City, Brooklyn, anger was there. I bounced in clubs in New York City while I was working my way through college, where there was also no shortage of anger. In all of my experiences, I learned. I watched. I experienced a lot of crazy and unsafe environments, did a lot of stupid and potentially lethal things, and survived, somehow.

I grew up in a small family, with my parents, Lloyd and Barbara, and my older sister, Alicia, who died when she was twenty. I was seventeen at the time, and it really fucked me up for a while, as it would virtually anyone. Knowing what it did to me, I think it destroyed my parents. How could it not?

Becoming an only child as a teenager sucked. The anger I already had become mixed with confusing, crushing grief. My devastated parents often looked far into the distance, or perhaps the past, as Alicia's future was taken and mine was yet to unfold. I watched them suffer powerlessly. I would sometimes chide them, that as terrible as it was that Alicia was gone, "I am still here" and needed them. They tried their best, under the most painful possible circumstances. Losing a kid is so unnatural, in so many ways. How does one ever actually recover? I've seen a lot of death in my life, but I don't think there's anything worse than burying your own child.

When the natural order of things gets thrown on its side and the world becomes more unpredictable, even for the most stable person, they become irritable, destabilized, and angry. It leaves people bracing for the next scary surprise and desperately trying to find the stability of confidence and the steady competence to navigate the world.

The paradox of losing my sister was piercing, because just when I started to feel confident again, as I came through the grief, I had my own children and realized, guess what? We're *always* vulnerable. As long as we love people, we're at risk of losing them. That can drive you mad if you let it. The best we can do is accept it and prepare ourselves and those around us. One thing I learned amid the simmering of my sister's and then my parents' deaths was that I would absolutely not go into the ground without the people around me knowing how I feel about them. If I love you, you know it. If you don't, that's not difficult to ascertain either.

Through these losses, I learned how important it is to be able to identify and name my feelings for people and demonstrate them. The pressure I felt to succeed—which had always been there—transformed after my sister's death, as I became an only child in a family shattered by loss. Suddenly, I was on a path to become a doctor, and in a struggling Jewish family, this meant something huge.

My father had grown up in the city's garment industry, when it was still a lucrative thing in the United States. He thought that he was going to inherit his father's business, which was successful, growing, and afforded them some luxury when my father was a kid. But not only did that *not* happen, when my father went into the business himself, following in his father's footsteps, he never rose above being a warehouse manager. This was not a glamorous, lucrative job, but one of millions of jobs that have virtually no upward mobility, and it meant living paycheck to paycheck. This meant that money was a *big* issue when I was a kid.

There was never enough, and we lived very modestly, surrounded by many other families who were also scraping to get by. My acquired taste for a big, thick steak, to some degree, was a reaction to having cheap, old chicken cooked every way my mother could think of. Out of necessity, she could stretch a quarter a mile. I was mad I couldn't have that steak as a child, and I can still conjure that feeling of frustration and anger, knowing it was out there, but beyond my reach at the time. I can still summon that feeling today, and it reminds me of why I work my ass off to avoid that feeling of inadequacy and having the "good stuff".

I was making more money working as a teenage lifeguard than my father ever made in any year of his life. This was not a small experience in my youth, because as we all know, money means opportunity. It means security, comfort, stability, and a kind of insulation from stress, fear, and anxiety that defines many people's lives. And there's more: While growing up as a poor child, poverty is humiliating, and humiliation hurts. I did not want this bad, gnawing feeling. This pain can very easily transform into anger, as anyone who has experienced it knows. Becoming a doctor was going to change this, but now, after Alicia's death, everything was different.

I didn't trust fucking doctors. Why would I? My sister had dropped dead at twenty. TWENTY!!! And the doctors couldn't prevent this? This did not compute. It really pissed me off, in the way grief mixed with deep anger does. I already had a kind of simmering resentment: I was poor, living as a minority in a neighborhood of minorities, and I had to defend myself all the time. I used the resentment I had as fuel. Even my best friends would tease me about being poor, or being Jewish, or any other stupid thing kids pick on one another for…and then, at times, turn on me.

I looked at my family and told myself: *I love my dad, and I want to be like him in many ways. But when it came to being financially successful and taking care of the family that way, he fell short. I'm not going to be poor like I was growing up. My kids are not going to be without, like I did. They're not going to feel this pain and embarrassment. Fuck this, I am getting out of here!*

There were many birthdays and Hanukkahs when I got nothing, and it made me feel like shit. I tried to adjust my expectations so that if I expected nothing, even a small something became a big deal. I learned to swallow these feelings of sadness and anxiety and just deal, but as anyone who has been there knows, this was very hard and painful.

I remember a guy going from place to place, selling little Matchbox cars that had probably "fallen off the truck," if you know what I mean. They were probably worth two dollars at the time, but my father could buy one for a quarter. He started bringing home some of these toys once in a blue moon, and to me, these tiny treasures were the equivalent of receiving a fucking Porsche. I was so grateful for something, even though it was smaller than small. It was never about my father not *wanting* to give. He did, and I could see and feel it. He was just not *able* to.

I watched him give something remarkable and invaluable instead: He found a way not to wear the stress of this poverty on the outside. He and my mother would talk about how they were going to afford food that week, and as she was stressed out, he would say, "Well, that's the adventure of it. We have to get creative." Instead of becoming angry or aggressive, he *lightened* it and tried to make her feel safe. My mother would have been just fine with a little less "adventure." She seemed to just feel the stress. It's also interesting to note that I never remember my mother having or showing any resentment toward my father and the financial situation she married into. They were always a team, which is such a testament to their resilience.

But for me, *poor* did not equate to *excitement*. It was very stressful, and as a little kid, that stress makes a knot in you, and you have no idea what to do with such feelings. Stress and anxiety can very easily become anger. My father told me a story when I was growing up, after we'd moved to Starrett City when I was four. Our car was stolen, and after that, we used public transportation until I eventually bought my own car. He told me about driving to work in his beaten, decrepit old car and pulling up at a red light, stressing to himself about money. Ordinarily, he would never admit he was worried, but he had one of those moments in life when the right person shows up exactly when you need them. He later told me he was thinking about how he was going to pay our bills, how he was going to keep it all together, and a Black man pulled up next to him, saw his anxiety in the broken-down, piece-of-shit car, and said, "Hey, man. Don't worry about it. It's just money," before driving away.

Retelling this story, my father swore that guy was an angel. No...like *really* an angel, as if he saw and felt what my dad was going through, like he was there to send him a message. He connected. He *lightened* the moment. He offered humanity and reflected back my father's ability to turn a shitty situation and stressful conditions into something he could live with.

I, however, was not as comfortable living with the stress. I was angry at a lot of things, but primarily, at the many things that were beyond my control. My sister's death amplified this. Losing someone makes a person feel powerless and heartbroken, and for me, anger was the emotion where all this sadness found a home. I was also starting to learn that when angry, I got stronger. I didn't yet understand the risk this represented, but I was starting to.

As a young athlete, I leaned into sports. I worked in a gym (Bally's Health & Fitness, formerly Jack LaLanne's, for any of my Brooklyn historians out there) as a lifeguard, and I quickly moved up to running the pools in Brooklyn. I was out-lifting the biggest guys, benching over four hundred pounds at the time, because I could summon this anger and lift more than I could in a non-angry state. I would recall an image of my sister in the hospital on the gurney after she died and imagined that somehow, if I made this lift, it would undo what had happened. That she would be back with us.

When I got myself into this frothy rage, I needed to take a little time to get it out of my system, but I could summon it when I needed it. I started to realize that this ability to call it up, use it, then be able to put it away was a *really* powerful ally, and I was learning how to use myself and my emotions to do what I wanted. Anger has a time and a place, and knowing where and when to use it is like holding the keys to the universe.

Eventually, I came to realize that, if harnessed, anger is like having a nuclear reactor in your belly that empowers you, keeps you going when others have quit. But there's more: When you're angry, you don't experience pain like you do when you're calm. That was a revolution for me. I can *engage* this shitty feeling and *direct* it? What? Things began to make much more sense, and I was on a path to understanding myself, and as it has turned out, thousands of people I've treated.

But how did I find this understanding? It was simple: by really letting anger consume and control me, by boiling over—exploding, really—and seeing what it did to the people I cared about. One day, when I was around thirteen or fourteen, I was hanging out in my room listening to my music. It was some really angry, thumping sound, which channeled right into my bloodstream, lathering me into a good, seething rage. I didn't realize my mother was knocking at my door, probably annoyed as hell about the volume and quality of music I was exposing her to.

She opened the door, startling me. I was already intense, but surprising me pulled the trigger, and I ripped a metal chair to shreds. You know, like the chairs WWE stars used to smash across each other's heads? Yeah, I tore it apart, like a beast. I will never forget the look on my mother's face, terrified and frozen. I had never seen her scared before, and *I* had done this to her. This was the only time I saw my mother terrified—not even on her deathbed.

Her words, spoken in fear, became a defining principle of my life: "You better get that shit under control or it's going to ruin your life." Simple as that. Control your anger *now*, or do nothing and it will *destroy* you. Without realizing it, this was the moment I began to understand anger management.

I knew I had to be very careful with the power this emotion can bring. It can help protect you and those around you. But anger can be terrifying, and for my own anger, this was news to me.

But I *wanted* to be scary. I wanted to be intimidating. I wanted to at least be *capable* of danger. It was a requirement of my Brooklyn neighborhood, and I didn't know another way, except for my father's ability to turn the bitterness of being poor into something lighter and less painful. I wasn't yet as evolved as he was, so vibrating at a frequency that transmitted *I can fuck you up* served me. I wanted the useful tool of anger to protect me, defend me, and make sure people knew I wasn't to be fucked with.

But the look on my mother's face in that moment, her pure terror, something I never saw before, changed me. As she said, "You better learn to put a lid on that or you're going to fuck up your whole life" (though she would never swear), she planted one of the most important seeds in my mind.

Learning about my own anger and my passion for sports and physical achievement, I began to pay attention to how athletes and coaches interact.

I often think of my friend Milton Love, who was on my Little League baseball team. I thought I was a better ballplayer than him, but I remember when he passed me like I was standing still. This kid was hitting 400-foot shots when he was fourteen. He was strong and fast and...challenging. Some coaches labeled him "uncoachable" even though he was one of the most respectful, well-raised kids in the neighborhood. Though he was a remarkable athlete, who I swore was going to play pro ball, his athletic career petered out in college. If coaches had a problem with Milton, they would definitely think everyone else in our neighborhood, or similar ones, was not worth the time and attention. I knew that somehow, something was wrong. Ideas began to take shape in me.

I started to think about how kids from the streets did not have the same opportunities, even well-behaved ones. And how, despite their talent, they would wind up down quicker paths because they weren't nurtured by coaches. I knew this had something to do with our "attitude," how we were perceived, and also how angry we all were about the unpredictable world we lived in.

I was surrounded by hardened kids, most of whom would never get to where they wanted to go. A lot of these kids were talented, but they were either chasing the quick money of drugs and gangs or they had temper problems and were getting arrested for getting into fights all the time. Nobody ever talked to them (or me) about the *strength* of control that was possible for them. They never had the benefit of learning about what can happen when their anger was channeled in the right direction, and this meant they were just loose cannons, capable of bursts of greatness but really messy in the background.

Everyone was just surviving, and my mother's words—"get that under control before it destroys you"—shone a light on the strength of control required to become a human Swiss army knife, in which the right tool only comes out under the right circumstances. There are times when anger is the ally you want. Yet, there are many more times that the strategic, cold move-maker, like those of Al Pacino's Michael Corleone in *The Godfather*, is the better way to go. The point is, anger, control, and aggression are all multifaceted, and there is a place for each if we know the difference.

It wasn't until I got older and was around some of the mob guys in the neighborhoods I frequented that I started to see that the really powerful people in my midst rarely got angry. They moved slowly, deliberately, like they were in total control of themselves and their environment. They would just make eye contact with you. They'd nod, you'd nod, and that was it. Everyone kept moving. Real power did not require an announcement or dramatic demonstration.

Or as one wise woman, La Wana Darden, later taught me: "My father used to say, 'The sun does not announce that it is rising.'" Meaning: people observe and take notice of power. If you have to demand that people know your power, you aren't doing it right. You don't actually have the power you think you do, and you're only fooling yourself.

I began to apply this lesson and this degree of control when I was bouncing in clubs, where people were hell-bent on losing their shit and getting out of control every night, like clockwork.

Watching that predictable mess every night at 2 a.m., I realized: You don't ever want to get angry when you're bouncing. Ever. *Everything* is about control. We're here to have a good time. If people around me were losing their shit, and they seemed programmed to act like idiots, I was not. My role was to remain calm and in control, no matter what. I was there to control their worst impulses, and it taught me more about *my* ability to modulate my responses to any situation.

As I went through school all over Brooklyn, my education on the street, in the gym, and at the clubs I worked in was as important as what I was learning in classrooms. Anger was everywhere, blowing up on the street day and night, and just ruining things, like the sports I was so committed to.

I hated when an athlete acted like an asshole, and it killed the team or the reputation of sports, like sports were the problem, not the player who couldn't keep themselves under control. Making matters worse, I found out the hard way that coaches usually would stoke the flames, activating already out-of-control athletes. Coaches want their team to play angry, until they're *too* angry and they make a mistake, and then they put their asses on the bench.

Coaches were often poor role models for anger management as well, hypocritically benching a player for losing their cool while the coach was yelling at the refs and players with such vigor, spittle flying out of their mouths. (And side note: Athletes want coaches whom they want to run through a wall for, not one you want to run through a wall to get away from.)

But no one ever taught the athletes how to manage this emotion. Anger management is not just about keeping your athletes eligible to play and out of jail. These tools are about performance enhancement, knowing how to get them up, really activating what motivates them to win, but also knowing how to get them down, back to a safe and socially stable level. This is like expertly stoking a fire: If you can't adjust the flame to that sweet spot, people are guaranteed to make mental mistakes that lead to losses. But also, a roaring fire of rage destroys people's lives.

Realizing this is when understanding anger really took off for me, and I saw a path forward as an expert in anger, working to help athletes succeed. Sport psychology was in its infancy, but there was obviously more need than there were people trained and available to do the work athletes, coaches, and the whole industry needed. Uncontrolled anger is all about emotional dysregulation, and I wanted to use my expertise to transform how we work with athletes, for whom becoming a warrior who wins is as much a mental game as it is physical.

Athletes know viscerally how primitively empowered one feels when they dominate another person.

I *was* an athlete. I understood this on a deep emotional level. I was also angrier—for good reason—than I wanted to be. I understood how to get in their heads. The "explosion threshold," as I like to call it, is very familiar to me, and it applies as easily in professional sport as it does in the prison populations I work with.

* * *

Think about it like this: Something happens, and it gets you really angry, and you have an opportunity to calm yourself back down *only* if you have the self-awareness and the skills to understand what the hell is happening with you. It's like if you're starting at one slightly amped up level, and then you get pissed off. You *could* go back down to baseline, but only if the conditions are right. And then something *else* happens, and you respond, and then you're at a higher level of anger. But it gets to a certain point when there's a straw that breaks the camel's back. At that point, you explode. To make matters worse, the thing that finally sets you off is usually a relatively minor thing, but because people didn't see the steps that got you angry, people around you think you're an idiot who's overreacting to nonsense. What they can't see is the "death by a thousand papercuts" that can lead someone to totally blow and lose their shit.

If you get to that point, to the explosion threshold, the only way you're going to resolve this emotional dysregulation is through physical restraint (a lot of it), through medication (a lot of it), or you let it run its course, which takes time. A lot of damage can happen before you run out of rage. Anger management is about preventing yourself from ever approaching the explosion threshold in the first place. You do so by getting ahead of the problem before the problem gets beyond your control. This applies to athletes just as much as it applies to people in prison, any boardroom in the country, and every other setting in between.

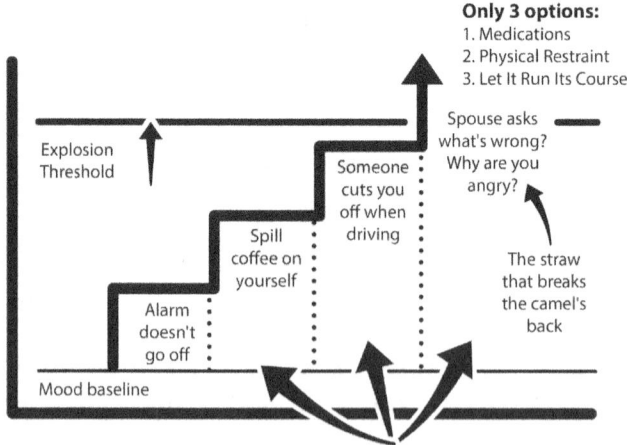

Each dotted line shows opportunities to de-escalate and get back down to baseline. However, because they did not do that, the stress accumulates and then they overreact to a relatively small thing.

On a very basic level, incarceration is about taking away people's rights because they broke laws, or taking nearly all control out of their hands. Prison is about rules, and virtually none of them are dictated by those inside. You don't get to shower whenever you want. You don't get to eat whatever or whenever you want. Your time belongs to the state, and there's no way around that. For people in jail, you either accept the fact that life is out of your control or you try to control what you can. Which is, by the way, what we tell athletes all the time: control the controllable, be where your feet are, and don't sweat the things that you can't control, because they will only distract you.

So what happens is: When you take people and you put them in an environment that limits their options, they're going to naturally try to find ways to feel powerful when their power is taken away. Nobody wants to feel inadequate. It sucks. But that's the irony of anger: If you can use your anger to be effective, bravo. If not, your emotion made you look like an idiot, screwed up your life, or put you in jail. That's not a fucking upgrade. Most people don't know when they've gone past the red line until it's already way too late. That's not the time to recognize you have issues with anger.

2

ANGER VS. AGGRESSION

So, what is anger management, exactly? The short answer is: It's *not* anger management. It's reactive aggression *prevention*.

"Anger management" implies that anger is a problem and you have to get rid of it. But no one gets in trouble for *being* angry. People get in trouble for the stupid shit that they *do* when they're angry. The higher the level of anger, the harder it is for us to make good decisions, which makes us more likely to do things that are hurtful to people and get us into trouble we can't walk away from.

This is very different from aggressiveness, which is a form of tenacity. It's the passion required to go after things, and the opposite of some kinds of aggression is passivity. No one has ever been successful by being completely passive and all soft, living entirely by the stupid *it's all good, man* mantra of burnouts. It's not all good, because many things require us to react appropriately, pursue them with intentionality and uniquely to each situation. Virtually nothing in life just drops into our lap. For sure, sometimes we need to be patient, and we definitely need good timing, in order for things to work out the way we truly want. But if you're just going to sit back and wait for success or the good stuff in life to drop in your lap, it's probably not going to happen. You have to go get it.

Successful people know that aggressiveness is a requirement, so we can't say that *all* aggression is bad. But what does that mean? Well, there are different types of aggression, like "goal-directed aggression," also called instrumental aggression, which is what it sounds like and is what we aim to maximize in our lives. That's when you're using your passion and your energy for a particular goal, like: I want to put the ball in the hoop. I want to hit my numbers this week in sales. I want to learn to play the violin. I want to get stronger, or faster, or more flexible. It means, "I want to *improve* and *achieve*" at something. It means actually *trying*. It doesn't mean no one ever gets hurt in instrumental aggression. It may happen, but it is a side effect, the unintended consequence, the collateral damage. Harming another is not the goal of instrumental aggression.

Then there is "reactive aggression." Reactive aggression is when someone has done something to you that you perceive as a harm or slight, and you react, and you want to hurt them, physically or emotionally, or you feel like slashing their tires. For reactive aggression, the goal is harm. For instrumental aggression, the goal is to reach a goal, *not* cause harm.

It doesn't mean that no one ever gets harmed in instrumental aggression, though. For example, when I was playing football, I would accept taking a penalty for laying someone out coming over the middle, in exchange for him worrying about me for the rest of the game. I did not *want* to hurt him. The goal was to make him afraid. If he got hurt, I could live with it, but it was deliberate to achieve my goal: impede his performance. With instrumental aggression, the primary goal is never to hurt someone else.

High levels of anger increase the likelihood of reactive aggres-sion, which should come as no surprise. But remember: You don't get in trouble for being angry. What we're trying to prevent is reactive *aggression*—and the destruction my mother was telling me to avoid. Decreasing the intensity of the emotions that feed reactive aggression is our goal to prevent problematic behaviors, like tearing chairs apart, or beating the hell out of someone and being charged with a crime.

To understand these concepts, it is helpful to understand the the-ories that were developed to help explain anger.

The first theory on anger management was called the Frustration Aggression Hypothesis, back in 1939. If you're frustrated or if some-body interferes with your goals, you're more likely to become violent. This makes sense. Then, in 1969, Leonard Berkowitz and his col-leagues came up with the Completion Hypothesis. This says that any "negative affect state" increases your likelihood of being violent immediately. On the one hand, this way of thinking is brilliant because it takes anger off the hook. Put another way, this theory says that if you're comfortable being angry, you're less likely to act out on it.

But why? Because you *understand* it. You could even argue that it's the irritability you experience from being angry that causes the vio-lence. So what Berkowitz was talking about and everybody can relate to is that if you're uncomfortable for any number of physical or emo-tional reasons, you can be very easily provoked. We've all experienced this. Hungry? You have a shorter fuse. Hence, being "hangry." Tired? Same. "Tangry." Burned out? It's easy to snap at people. Scared? Fighting makes sense.

Early on, experts didn't even want to talk about the psychodynamic stuff and the trauma carried by some people who are experiencing anger, but this is important to point out. In many cases, anger is a reaction to trauma, and you can't really treat the anger until you treat the trauma. In fact, I would even say that for people who have trauma histories, I often *prescribe* the anger rather than just waiting for it to happen. Huh? Why would I do that, and what does this mean? Sometimes, accessing one's anger can help someone recover from trauma, because it helps them feel less powerless. Anger can feel proactive, protective, and better than feeling the pain of trauma, but getting to the anger requires some work, digging, and that can be painful, at least at first.

Trauma is about avoidance. It's like saying, "Bad shit happened to me, so I have to run away from it." I say: Stop running. You can't outrun your demons. Attack them. Fight back, emotionally. Fight for yourself. Getting angry about what happened to you helps you fight. The psychological argument for saying "get super fucking pissed about this" is: As long as you're symptomatic after a traumatic event (and many people don't realize they are), the person/event/thing or circumstance that hurt you continues to win. To my patients for whom I help to access their anger, I say: Aren't you fucking tired of that? Embrace the anger and use it when this treatment is hard. Find the anger and use it as a way to protect yourself, and once you feel better, we will work to keep the anger at a level that protects you.

The ideas that came together to become what we call anger management really took off in the '80s, and by the time I got into it in the 1990s, there was no one in sports doing what I was doing. This allowed me to become an expert quickly, because so few people were looking at athletics through the lens of anger.

And for those readers out there thinking, *I'm not an athlete, I'm not reading this from prison, and I'm not even angry*, I say this: You may not be angry right now, but you have been, and you will be again. This *does* apply to you.

When I first wanted to help athletes better manage their anger, most coaches shut the door on me, afraid I'd turn their teams into a bunch of wusses. They didn't yet understand that this emotion is a powerful tool that can be accessed and used. It was an uphill battle to get coaches to understand that, contrary to "softening" their athletes, this would strengthen them and give them superior mastery over their emotions. What I do has the potential to turn them into better performers, better teammates, and better humans. My goal was to use what is already in them, anger, and turn it into a superpower.

I realized that there were a lot of athletes who weren't going as far as they could because of anger and criminal issues. When I was getting ready to apply to graduate school, I had a professor who told me I'd never be a psychologist. *Fuck you. Watch me!* I thought. Nothing's more motivating than when someone tells you that you can't achieve something, dismissing and minimizing you. It pisses you off. It activates you. It *angered* me. After many applications and interviews, I landed at Long Island University, and the person who became my mentor was Eva Feindler.

At the time, Dr. Eva Feindler was the top anger management expert in the world for children and adolescents. I had an idea. I wanted to take her program and apply it to athletics. In fairness, some of the reasons I wanted to do this weren't just because of my intimate relationship with anger in sports. I also hated when an athlete acted like an asshole and damaged how people perceived sport, and talked shit about it, like being an athlete was a bad thing. So, admittedly, some of my intention was that I was going to ride in on a white horse and help athletes not act like assholes. I believed that the coaches were going to be happy about it, like I'd solved a problem that no one could figure out, or hadn't thought about in the right way.

Then I found out the hard way that coaches often want players to be total assholes. They want athletes to play angry until they're too angry, and when they make a mistake, they put their asses on the bench. But no one ever taught them how to manage their emotions. And no one ever taught the coaches how to coach this aspect of performance well. It wasn't until I was able to repackage anger as totally normal and actually controllable that I began to make some inroads with coaches. Anger management is not just about keeping your athletes eligible to play and out of jail. It is also about performance enhancement. You know how to get them up, but you don't know how to get them down. And if you can't adjust that flame to that sweet spot, you're going to have mental mistakes.

This was when things began to take off. Eva, my mentor, liked my approach but said I needed to go find a sport psychologist. At this time, around 1995, I had never heard of a sport psychologist, and there were no sport psychology programs in schools that I was aware of. Eva sent me in search of someone named Shane Murphy at a massive conference of students, professors, and professionals in sports. She told me to see if I could find him. "Tell him what you're planning to study and research for your dissertation (applying her anger management program to athletes), and see what he thinks." Dr. Murphy was the first full-time sport psychologist for the United States Olympic Committee.

I said, "Eva, there are going to be thousands of people there. How the hell am I going to find him?" She said, "You're going to do what you do. You're going to figure it out." As fate would have it, he just sat down right next to me. And, though he's Australian, he's a Mets fan, like me. We connected immediately. And as soon as I told him what my idea was, he responded, "Great, mate, let's do it." Simple as that.

That moment in time is what set my path to be a sport psychologist. If Shane did not respond the way he did, with enthusiasm, encouraging my idea, I would not be where I am now. And in turn, I have always made myself available to students and young professionals, lending a hand, giving some direction, and introducing them to the right people. It is how I pay forward what Shane did for me.

As he began mentoring me, with his expertise at the top of the mountain of sports, with his experience with the Olympic teams, my ideas about anger and athletics became formalized. Shane gave me the confidence I needed, and a kind of permission that my perception of anger in the sport psychology world was 100 percent valid and could add real value.

3

REWRITING THE DICTIONARY

I was already treating inpatient adolescents, personality disordered adults, and then chronically mentally ill patients in a state mental hospital, and I had seen a great deal of anger turned inward, as well as externalized. I was the Senior Psychologist at Coney Island Hospital in Brooklyn for a while, where patients came right off the streets in the most dire of life and psychiatric circumstances. Many had been literally through hell and had never received a moment of help.

They came from all walks of life and represented every demographic. But what they had in common was that they were either physically or mentally ill—and both, in many cases. Anger was a part of every day in that hospital. People were scared, miserable, and in desperate need of care. And since, for twenty-five years, I've worked with inmates in the state prison system in New Jersey, some with the most severe criminal histories society has to offer. They are serial killers, gang members, hitmen, legitimately psychotic patients, psychopaths, sex offenders, and everything else you can imagine.

You know what they all have in common? They're all human. And, as part of being human, they have emotions, including—you guessed it—anger. They don't all experience anger the same way and certainly don't share the same behavioral repertoire in response to rage, but to lesser or greater degrees, one of the themes I've come to appreciate is that those who cannot modulate their anger effectively will consistently fall short of their life goals.

In fact, the first week I was working at Northern State Prison, I met Dr. Harold Goldstein (who now has about forty years of correctional experience). He has become one of my closest friends and most respected colleagues. I learned a ton from him over the decades, but at that point, we didn't know each other. We were new colleagues. He had been there for a while, and I was just starting, coming from Coney Island Hospital. We quickly started a conversation about what commonality most of these inmates had, and we joined immediately around the premise that emotional dysregulation, the struggle with managing one's emotions, including anger, was the central theme that most incarcerated people struggled with.

For some of my clients, their life goal is to win a championship. For others, it's to stay out of the revolving door of recidivism and never get locked up again. Anger management is a skillset that *all* people can benefit from; it's just that some are born with a better toolkit. Some learn it along the way. But you show me someone with a barren anger management toolkit, and I'll show you someone with areas of their lives in which they are losing.

But let's take a step back for a moment. Even though I'm an anger management expert, I'm not a hypocrite. Or at least, I try really hard not to be. That is to say that just because I've been doing this work for a long time, it doesn't mean that if you followed me around, you wouldn't find me losing my mind from time to time, irritable and grumpy, snapping disproportionately at fairly innocuous situations. Zero incidents of this sort is aspirational, but most of us never get there, which is entirely natural. We all make mistakes, so as long as our mistakes are recoverable, this is how we learn and find the richness in life. These mistakes, what we learn, and how we recover are where our wisdom comes from. It's like our awareness muscles are being strengthened. However, the more we're aware and open to understanding our specific process—how we deal with situations that provoke us; how we recognize our triggers and are willing to "own our shit"—the better we'll be at learning and continuing to improve our personal effectiveness.

Wisdom is what we should aspire to. It is accumulated knowledge and experience. But, as the saying goes, "youth is often wasted on the young." The impetuous exuberance runs hither and yon, missing the lessons that can be accumulated. Yet, wisdom requires self-awareness, confidence, humility, and patience. Wisdom helps us understand that sometimes the best reaction is no reaction. My hope is that this book helps you accelerate your journey toward wisdom.

What does this all mean? You didn't come here to read my resume. My professional experience is very rare, and it affords me a view of our society—and the role anger plays in it—that virtually no one else has. The truth is that most people struggle with anger, and even more importantly, *everyone* gets angry, for different reasons, under different circumstances, and to different degrees. We all have different boiling points and life challenges each of us in different ways. While my goal is to provide greater understanding and tools on how to manage our anger, a person's individual struggles, factors, history, and perspectives on the world all are going to require deeper analysis than can be done in a book.

So, now you have a bit of a new perspective on anger. You can see it the way I do: as just another emotion, neither good nor bad, and just a part of being human. At this point, I'd like for you to assess your own relationship or experience with anger. Think about it in your own life. Are you even aware of how much anger you feel? Is it a low, gentle, and constant simmer? Or, is it a robust boil? For a few of you out there, is it a white-hot, incandescent blaze that can be blinding? It's going to be different for everyone, but there is some degree of anger in every single person. That is totally normal. Perhaps consider why you picked up this book in the first place. You know somewhere in there, you're angry about some things, and you hope to improve how you respond, harnessing it to help you get where you want to go, rather than sabotaging yourself.

If you're having such difficulties with extreme anger that it's leading to behaviors that you haven't been able to tame, and you're dealing with severe consequences, don't expect this book to be able to replace psychotherapy. I would encourage you to explore your therapeutic options, because I'm convinced that everyone, at some time in their life, could benefit from psychotherapy, whether it's to treat a specific problem or to gain a greater understanding of their whole, existential self. Finding this way of living, in which you find meaning and your own path to self-actualization, matters, because, trust me, it will make you happier.

* * *

Anger. Aggressiveness. Violence. Hostility. These words are used almost interchangeably. Before I wrote my book in 2010, *Anger*

Management in Sport: Understanding and Controlling Violence in Athletes, I searched the psychological literature because the terminology that was used didn't make any sense to me. For example, aggression was defined by actions that had, as its primary goal was to harm another person. This baffled me. Why? Because every interview I've ever heard with a successful person talks about them being aggressive, even though they've never hurt a fly.

Anger has been nearly exclusively defined as a negative emotion, though people have only recently begun to appreciate the facilitative nature anger can have. However, it's still nearly always demonized for its risks, which people believe outweigh its benefits. It sounded like some kind of poison that had to be exorcised from your soul. It was seen to be the cause of great torment and injury to others, and it could lead to all kinds of medical problems, like hypertension, immune suppression, acceleration of cardiac disease, ulcers...you name it. If an illness can be impacted by stress, anger has been considered a cause. There was practically nothing "good" said about anger anywhere.

Guess what? Many of the people I've met in prison who were violent were not even angry at the time of their crime. That's right. There are people who have engaged in severe violence who were not angry at the time that they did so. What does this tell us? The old definitions are obsolete, useless, and don't do anything to help us understand anger and how it presents itself on a day-to-day basis.

The definitions that follow, I hope, are vast improvements over the antiquated terms that not only have been proliferating in psychological literature for years, but continue to be misunderstood and misused by all of us.

ANGER

Anger is a neutral emotion, neither good nor bad. It's associated with a spike in your sympathetic nervous system (a physiological escalation, which we'll get to later) and is often in response to a perceived threat or affront that may be conscious or unconscious. The thoughts associated with the emotion focus on attacking or confronting the irritant, and the behavior tends to follow suit. Behaviors associated with anger often include, but are in no way limited to: yelling, throwing things, threatening, using profanity or sarcasm, and at times becoming physically violent.

It's critical to understand that there is no mandatory connection between the *experience* of anger and a behavioral *response*. For example, you could be stewing about something right now, but I wouldn't know that because there's no change in your facial expression, no yelling or change in your voice or the speed and pitch of your speech, and no behavioral analog at all. I know that the better someone becomes at being aware of their emotions and choosing how to act on them (or not), the more personal power they are commanding and transmitting.

Anger is one of our six primary emotions, which arises directly from a situation. All of our primary emotions—happiness, sadness, fear, disgust, surprise, and anger—are hardwired into our physiology, and we feel them.

This has to be repeated. One of the biggest problems people have with anger is that they presume that there's a required behavioral response that always coexists with a feeling of anger, leading them to feel like they are absolutely required to act. This is just not true. I don't know anybody on the planet who doesn't get angry. Granted, some people are more physiologically prone to anger, or their triggers are easier to access than others, but I have no doubt that if you put Mother Teresa in a Department of Motor Vehicles waiting room, you're going to see an angry person... And there is nothing wrong with that. We all know the feelings of frustration that come with life, and feelings of frustration can quickly lead to anger. But what we do next is what we're talking about, and why you're here.

As we just discussed, the Frustration-Aggression Hypothesis explained that people are more likely to become violent when they're frustrated as well as when someone or something interferes with their goal. It's easy to wrap your head around how and why, and it makes sense, right? We all get pissed off when someone gets in our way as we're trying to do something, but in fact, when people are asked to describe their anger in these moments, they usually describe their frustration instead, because their anger got in their way. Did anger make anything move faster at the DMV? No. Did a road rage-induced temper tantrum make the slow-as-shit driver ahead move faster? No. So, anger, in these moments, served no purpose.

If you want to get through the DMV quicker, you're not going any faster by throwing a temper tantrum, right? Or, if you're late and behind a slow-as-shit driver, tailgating will do nothing for you. You can always pull over to the side and have a fight, if you want, but why would you? You'll be even later, right? And adding anger to frustration just makes your life and other people's lives harder. Yes, people are more likely to become violent when they're frustrated, which is obvious and internally consistent, but it's a waste of your energy. Don't bother allowing your frustration to boil over into anger, because frustration passes, and your angry response will define the situation, even if you feel your anger is warranted.

And, the Completion Hypothesis predicted that as we learn to understand what pisses us off and what we do about it. Simply put, you're more likely to be aggressive during any negative affect state. This refers to any time you're experiencing unpleasant emotions, like sadness, anxiety, fear, guilt, stress, shame, envy, or anger. Now, I don't think of anger as a negative affect state, but this hypothesis classifies emotions as negative or positive. What I see is that any emotional or physical condition that leads us to be irritable makes us more aggressive. But here's the point: Irritability passes quickly. We're so adjustable and so easily irritated, we can quickly move through these feelings fast, without having strong reactions. We're basically built to be cranky. Being tired, hungry, cold, overworked, bored, lonely, anxious, and surrounded by too many people who piss us off and just living in the world brings all of our sensitivities to the surface.

The Completion Hypothesis is also the basis of the concept we have of being "hangry"—more angry when we are hungry. But, there is also "tangry"—more irritable when we are tired. "Sangry," grumpy when we are sick. Anyone who ever had the flu and overreacted when someone brought them a nice cup of Jewish penicillin (chicken soup), feeling their words on their skin like fingernails on a chalkboard, knows exactly what I mean. When we feel off, we are more likely to snap at people.

To this, I say: Learn what these feelings are, and put them in their proper context. Virtually none of this will kill you, so give it a few minutes, eat something, or put a sweater on, and chances are that you'll feel better. Get a good night's sleep and you are guaranteed to feel better tomorrow. Take some time to take care of yourself and you'll see how quickly much of your irritability passes. It's almost impossible to know how you feel when you're exhausted and depleted, which makes naming your emotions so much harder and increases the chances of getting it wrong.

This point was driven home for me while I was working with an Olympic gymnast. She reminded me of the important lesson in celebrating our victories, no matter how small they may seem. Our mental health, and our ability to regulate our emotions and not just reach for anger at the drop of a hat, is crucial to learning when to be happy, just as importantly as when we're about to get really pissed off and regret it. I asked this young woman, who had trained with some of the Eastern European coaches with well-known abusive styles, how she had survived her experience. She didn't seem psychologically damaged by her experience, though others on her team had been permanently scarred by what they had gone through.

What she said was truly brilliant. She told me that once she realized that some of the people around her were just bad people, that they would hurt anyone, she began to question why they were in their leadership roles. She realized that they were in charge because they were the best in the world at the technical side of the sport, but they lacked the other parts that made them fully human. So you know what she did? She learned to *turn off the volume* on them and just *listen for the correction*. She learned to listen for the lesson in what they were saying to her, even though they were saying it with a maximum of shittiness. Having learned to do that, she could apply the lesson and improve as an athlete. As long as she wasn't destroyed by the volume they were using on her, she was able to get better and better, without absorbing their nastiness.

For those of us who are not part of an abusive Olympic team, the lesson is the same: try to hear the positive in the stream of shitty coming our way, so we can react without overreacting. Because if we're not careful, the negative we see, hear, feel, experience, and how we react to it overshadows any benefit we get from all of the good in our lives.

Okay, so this may sound like total bullshit, and you may be thinking that I don't know your life, and how much frustrating and stressful shit happens, and how it's a miracle you haven't lost your shit and told everyone to go to hell. I'm telling you that regardless of what's happening in your life, there is more good than bad. Remember: I treat incarcerated men and women who have had nearly *all* choices taken from them. We have a choice in terms of how we react, and a former gymnast reminded me that we can lower the volume on what we don't like so that we don't spin out of control.

Another thing we can do is improve how we buttress and build how we praise other people, so when we have something harsh to say, we don't attack other people's character, which just makes them fucking angry and repeats the whole cycle. Parents know this. There's a huge difference between saying "What you did sucked" and saying "You're a bad kid." But the same works on adults. Say what you need to say, but say it in a way that wouldn't cause you to feel like shit if you were hearing it.

This leads to "modeling," which goes one way or the other. People are either teaching us what to do or what not to do. We're all either prone to repeating what we've seen *or* we're going to fix it. Modeling is what we see around us, especially how people manage their emotions. Modeling is so important for emotional intelligence because it teaches us to read people. It makes us smarter, safer, and more able to anticipate how other people feel rather than just reacting, and it teaches us to identify how we feel, in different circumstances. It shows us that there are actual threats, and when we know what they are, we can move around them, rather than living in an illusion of safety and control, which is much more dangerous.

The Completion Hypothesis reminds me of a client of mine who was referred to my practice to learn some anger management skills. He's a giant person, six-foot-four, maybe 270 pounds of strength. He recently told me about a road rage incident he handled really well—and differently than he might have done prior to our work together. He wasn't sure when the change took place in him, but he said he finally realized that any time he's in an interaction that leads to heightened emotions, someone could die. If he punches someone, and they fall and hit their head, he is capable of delivering deadly strength that could end someone's life.

Think about what he was saying here. He identified the difference between bending versus breaking, and anger plays a crucial role here. Most of us never know when we're on the verge of breaking something that can't be repaired. We talk about this in prison all the time, and for some of the incarcerated men and women I treat, they can only identify the moment in which they broke something when it was too late. They had reached their breaking point and were paying the price. I say that we win 100 percent of the fights we avoid, because the truly horrific negative consequences that could happen don't matter if the fight is avoided.

To be 100 percent clear, there are some fights that can't be avoided. I never advocate for taking a beating, and people should know how to defend themselves. But if there is no alternative but to engage in a physical fight, be fast, decisive, and get the fuck out of the situation as quickly as possible. I learned to fight young, and though it's ancient history now, I learned to say, "This is not going to end well for you, so why don't we both just walk away?" I don't care if people think I'm a pussy; being able to walk away physically unharmed and without having allowed my anger to boil over is a victory.

Some people think that anger management and learning to control our anger is learning to be meek, and getting comfortable with taking shit from people, but nothing could be farther from the truth. In fact, yes, anger management is a way of learning the soft skills of dealing with other people that many of us don't get through the modeling of our parents or environments. But soft skills are much more important than hard skills because it's our soft skills that allow us to adapt. And adapting is what matters, because learning to understand your emotions and controlling them rather than being controlled by them is the road to success.

Now, I grant you, this is easy to say and can be hard to do. We live in overwhelming and exhausting times, leading many people to feel emotionally and mentally drained and constantly stressed. This cognitive fatigue makes processing nearly every situation harder, leading to overreacting when there's nothing worth reacting to. When we get overwhelmed, we have more difficulty filtering out the things that don't matter, and our defenses go down. Things that shouldn't matter get inside our heads, and they pile up as we become more overwhelmed. But the more you're able to pay attention to your own emotional state and identify your triggers, the more you're able to just let nearly everything slide off you. This makes getting angry seem stupid, like you reacted to the psychological noise of the world that you would have been better off just muting.

What about when anger *is* a secondary emotion, or a response to being hurt, upset, scared, ashamed, or anxious? I've spent a fair amount of time pointing out that anger is not a secondary emotion. This is because many people, including experts, have argued that anger is not a primary emotion. I call bullshit on that. However, I would be remiss to not also acknowledge that anger can be a secondary emotion, and that deserves to be discussed and explored a bit.

If it is secondary, what is it secondary to? What is the initial feeling or experience that someone has prior to anger? Most often, it is a feeling of hurt or being slighted or embarrassed. It's not surprising then that anger can help us recover from that. Rather than having a bruised ego or being left feeling fragile, anger can rile us up, help us feel powerful, and prompt us to go do something to someone who hurt us.

That said, anger may be a distraction or, even worse, an emotion that stimulates vengeance. While evening the score might have some momentary appeal, it doesn't undo what happened to you. And, left as is, you're stuck with your injuries, whether they are physical, emotional, or something that feels like a piece of your soul was ripped from you.

Should you forgive? Perhaps. Should you forget? Fuck that. Let's explore each of these a bit more.

I think the question of forgetting when someone has done you dirty is easier to answer. Simply, the answer is no. The best predictor of future behavior is past behavior. If you don't take note of when someone has harmed you, you are prone to being harmed again. Hence the saying, "Fool me once, shame on you. Fool me twice, shame on me."

Yet, choosing not to forget something does not mean it has to weigh on you like an anvil around your neck. Many people waste a lot of energy carrying around grudges (which are a bit of both—not forgiving or forgetting). I see grudges as parasites, vestigial reminiscences that suck the energy out of you and provide little value. You can remember who did you wrong and how, and be even more cautious around them or the familiar triggers to the event, without being hypervigilant and letting it consume you. Thinking about it practically, if you stay invested in everyone and everything that ever hurt you, you will become increasingly closed off from the world, agoraphobically locked in your room to prevent anything from happening to you. Fuck that. Learn the lessons. Have them accessible. But don't let anything that happened to you dictate your future trajectory.

And then there's forgiveness. Forgiveness is tricky. And heavy. And complex. Often, people want to talk about forgiveness with such a superior, morally enlightened, and religious righteousness. I don't want to go too far astray as I am not a theologian. Yet, there are certainly some good psychological concepts embedded in the process of Christian forgiveness. I'm not all in on the idea that if people don't forgive others, God will not forgive them. And I'm not a big believer in unconditional love. I think the closest we get to that is with our children, and they push those limits at times anyway. Marriage? Marital vows exist *because* there are conditions.

However, I like the idea that people (Christians) are called to forgive others regardless of whether they deserve it or they repent. Not because we must mirror God's supposed unconditional love, but because it's good for you. Because forgiveness means releasing the bitterness and desire for revenge, it's a necessary step toward personal healing and the restoration of relationships.

Judaism offers some useful psychological guidance as well. In

Judaism, forgiveness is a fundamental part of human relationships and a duty that is mentioned in the Torah. It's a way to restore integrity and dignity, and to emulate God's mercy and kindness. It's also about taking ownership. One has the duty to seek forgiveness for harmful actions and should atone for them. There is appreciation that forgiveness takes time, but it's a way one can restore integrity and dignity. Forgiveness requires self-examination, owning one's actions, expressing regret, attempting to right the wrong, and moving on.

It's worth noting that an apology without a change in behavior is the ultimate "fuck you." If you apologize, there's an expectation that you won't repeat what you did. In fact, there are a lot of expectations, and that's why apologizing can sometimes be the worst thing you could do to someone. What?! Huh? I know!!! You're scratching your head thinking, *Apologizing is exactly what you do when you hurt someone.* Let me point out the problem here.

Let's say I punch you in the nose. Would it hurt? You're goddamned right it would.

Now, what does society expect me to do?

Apologize.

And then what is expected of you, the one who got slugged in the schnozz?

Forgive me.

Yeah, but your nose still fucking hurts.

That's the problem. The apology shifts the onus onto the victim of what they are supposed to do. What if they're not ready for an apology? What if it still hurts? And they don't want to forgive right now?

That's the issue. After you do something, you want to apologize and be taken off the hook. Forgiveness is a gift to someone who hurt you, but a gift that does not have to be given. I think someone needs to think really hard if they are ready to move on from something.

Don't apologize if you don't mean it.

Don't accept an apology if you're not ready. Because if you do, you're saying you're over it, which you really may not be.

It comes up a lot in my work with patients and clients. When someone has done something to hurt you, the truth is, they can never undo what has happened. And neither can you. Only you can decide if it will become a part of your past or remain in the future, impacting your life and possibly changing your future.

Even more powerful is that once you have forgiven someone, you no longer rent out space to that person in your head. They don't have to have any influence. You can forgive them and decide you won't ever give them another chance to hurt you.

You can deliberate with yourself how they may have helped you by learning a life lesson. Or found out who they truly are.

So yes, anger can sometimes blind us from our hurt. It could be a way to protect ourselves from being hurt again. But forgiveness? Well, forgiveness is a gift that we don't just give the offender. It is a gift we give ourselves when we are ready to free ourselves from the emotional baggage, learn our lessons, lick our wounds, and move forward tougher and wiser. Hopefully, without anger.

4

HOW DO WE DEAL WITH AND <u>USE</u> ANGER?

We put entirely too many demands on people and how they're supposed to feel. "You should feel this way." Or "You shouldn't feel that way. You're reading the situation wrong. You're overreacting." Or "That's nothing to be angry about. Why are you angry?"

Now do you understand why you get the response, "I'm not fucking angry"? Have you ever heard somebody respond, "Well, I've been having a really bad day today. My car wouldn't start, I spilled coffee all over myself, my husband was nagging me, and my boss had no patience for me being late, so those are the reasons I am angry...at least the reasons that I am aware of at the moment."

If somebody responded to your question regarding their perceived anger that way, you would probably respond more compassionately and may ask them if there was anything you could do to help. The problem with it all is that asking why you are angry sounds like an accusation, since we all subconsciously know that showing anger is often a buzzkill, and it's sometimes perceived as aggressive or antisocial. It sounds like an accusation. People then respond defensively. We don't give people the space to feel the way they feel, especially when anger is in the middle of it.

There is no way that anybody is going to learn how to manage their anger until they feel safe and comfortable enough that they can admit that it's there and do something about it.

AGGRESSION

Aggression is the tenacity with which someone goes after their goals. Aggressiveness, which is the adverb describing behavior, captures this best. There can be a misunderstanding when we describe someone as aggressive. People might mistakenly think that it means that they're violent, though I believe it's a subset of the several types of aggressiveness possible. To break it down simply, there are two types of aggression: instrumental aggression and reactive aggression.

Instrumental aggression, sometimes called "goal-directed aggression," is when somebody is pursuing their goal with great passion, enthusiasm, or intensity in order to increase the likelihood of achieving that goal. A secondary consequence of that behavior may be to harm someone, but it is not the goal. An example of this would be a basketball player heading to the hoop in order to score. In the process of driving the lane, they accidentally elbow an opponent in the face. There is no denying that the other player got hurt, but that was not the goal. The goal was to put the ball in the hoop.

Another example may be a young executive, in the process of trying to impress her bosses, who utilizes unconventional tactics to increase her clientele. Her increased status leads clients of one of her coworkers to choose to transfer to her accounts. Her goal was to increase her sales. She had no intention of hurting her colleague, but nonetheless he clearly was. Again, it's not that no one can get hurt in instrumental aggression; it is that hurting someone is not the goal. I know that people who are successful maximize instrumental aggression and minimize reactive aggression.

You may sometimes hear people interchange instrumental aggression with assertiveness. They are not the same.

Assertiveness refers to a communication style in which you stand up for your rights. Assertiveness training is something that therapists do with individuals with low self-esteem who don't advocate for themselves. While it's important to be assertive, it should not be used synonymously with instrumental aggression because people are simply afraid to admit that they are aggressive.

Not to mention the fact that if you want to be successful in life, assertiveness is only going to get you so far. Let's go to the soccer field for an example. Is the attacker really going to say, "Excuse me, Mr. Goalie, could you kindly move out of the way because I have the right to score a goal now and I want to kick it past you..."? Of course not! That's ridiculous. You have no "right" to score a goal. A player will do so aggressively, or not at all.

Assertiveness skills are taught in anger management, especially for folks who have been angry and unsuccessful in their communication patterns in the past, but it would be a mistake to equate assertiveness with aggressiveness.

Further, the assertiveness training is to help folks maximize their effectiveness. It teaches you to stand up for yourself by using verbal skills to achieve your goals. This includes picking the right time and right place and "plating the meal" in a manner that will get you in the best mindset to listen and give you what you want.

Reactive aggression, which is similar to hostile aggression, is behavior that has as its primary and sometimes solitary goal to do harm to someone. Reactive aggression is related to anger and often is the behavior that leads people to get into trouble. Reactive aggression is usually implemented in response to a perceived injustice, insult, or wrongdoing. A sports example of this would be an offensive lineman trash-talking a defensive lineman about his mother, saying obscene things. Furious, the defensive lineman gets up and smacks the offensive lineman in the helmet, incurring a 15-yard penalty and being ejected from the game. Note, this was in reaction to a provocation, which is why it's called reactive aggression.

Hostile aggression is not in response to anger or a provocation, but does have as its primary goal: to harm someone else. This comes from the individual's temperament, irritation, belief that they can impose their will (some of the factors in the hostility bias), but is not in response to the recipient's wrong-doing. When you see prevalent hostile aggression by an individual or a group, it means they embrace the acceptance of violence as a way to do business.

So, instrumental aggression paves the way for success, while reactive aggression paves the way for trouble. Why? People, especially men, are very sensitive to issues of power. If you say the right thing at the right time and you can provoke somebody to fight, you control them. The toughest guy in prison doesn't have to fight. Nobody wants to fight him. And because they're secure in their power, they're not easily provoked. If you're someone who wears your emotional buttons on your sleeve, can be easily provoked, and often engage in reactive aggression, you are also someone who gives your power away all the time.

Think about it like this: Real power is like being Teflon; nothing sticks to you and nothing breaks you. One of the biggest problems with chronic anger is that you can easily be taken down a path that will harm you. That is why you don't want anger to be too high. That is why you want to learn how to prevent reactive aggression.

VIOLENCE

Violence can be most easily defined as an extreme form of reactive aggression. Like mentioned above, however, not all violence occurs when people are angry. Predatory violence, for example, requires the exact opposite physiological process as being in a rage. When people or animals are hunting, they are silent, decisive, thinking clearly, and absolutely goal-directed. The panther that hides in the brush waiting for its prey to wander close enough to be ambushed is clearly not angry or out of control. Similarly, psychopathic serial killers, even while violent, don't have the increase in heart rate or sympathetic nervous system activity that you normally would find with someone when they're angry. One could even say that predatory violence is instrumental aggression, where the goal is to harm someone.

Most commonly, however, violence is connected with extreme anger, and the goal is to harm someone. The method of harm can take several forms, and it is also important to consider behavior within societal norms. For example, fighting in hockey is not seen as violence, exactly, because the rules don't sanction it severely and a referee waiting to break up the fight speaks to a complicit acceptance of fighting. From this perspective, fighting in hockey is not necessarily violence. Terry and Jackson (1985) defined sports violence as "harm-inducing behavior outside the rules of sport, bearing no direct relationship to the competitive goals of sport." This provided a useful perspective to determine what constitutes violence in sports and what doesn't.

Here's another example: sparring in boxing. Now, some may say that boxing, by definition, *is* fighting, but when both parties are wearing headgear and the goal is to perfect timing, technique, and execution, it's easier to see that this is not violence either.

HOSTILITY

If anger is an *emotion* and aggression is a *behavior*, with aggressiveness being an adverb, hostility is more of a personality trait, a longer-standing pattern of behavior. Hostility can be thought of as a condition of chronic anger. Remember that we discussed that anger is normal and that we all get angry from time to time. Well, have you ever noticed that some people tend to wake up on the wrong side of the bed every goddamn day? These folks carry hostility around with them as their baseline and often have a distorted view of the world, known as a "hostility bias."

Embedded in the hostility bias are four common cognitive problems or distortions:

COGNITIVE DISTORTION	EXAMPLE
1. Tendency to perceive neutral stimuli as provocative.	*Johnny is walking down the hall in high school and accidentally bumps into Chris. Chris starts yelling at Johnny, asking him why he deliberately bumped into him.*

2. Difficulties identifying non-hostile explanations for an event.

When Chris is asked if there could be any other explanations for why Johnny bumped into him, Chris' response is, "Nope, that asshole did it on purpose."

3. Difficulties generating solutions to situations that don't involve violence.

Chris is asked about the different ways that he could have perceived or handled the situation, but he is "stumped." He has great difficulties understanding any possible way to handle things besides using violence.

4. Legitimization of violence. It is not just that they have difficulties generating non-violent responses, but they believe violence is the justified, recommended response to perceived injustice. Might is right.

Chris not only uses physical violence as his go-to problem solver, but he believes it is the best way to handle things. You will sometimes hear people say things like, "Yeah, well, when I kick your ass, you won't fuck with me again."

What are the good and the bad about the hostility bias? The bad news is that it's pretty obvious that these ways of thinking are taught to kids, through the modeling they get from parents, peers, and the media. Similar to racism (and every other -ism, for that matter), these views of the world are narrow-minded and not very pragmatic for a successful life, but because they are ingrained in children from a very young age, they often see this view of the world as innate and natural.

Not surprisingly, many bullies embrace this cognitive framework. Why do bullies continue? Often, psychologists try to give complicated explanations, like they are externalizing their trauma from being bullied themselves, or they struggle with low self-esteem and will harm others to feel more powerful. While these deep conceptualizations may have some legitimacy, there is a much more basic reason why this pattern continues: because it works. For example, if I beat you up and take your lunch money, I enjoy having your money, and I will continue to do this until there is a good reason not to.

When the reward structure changes, the behavior changes. When the bully gets his ass handed to him, or his parents severely punish him for his behavior, then his behavior may change. Until then, the bullying behavior is reinforced, and it will continue...as does the cycle of the hostility bias. People are unlikely to take a look at their view of the world until they face consequences that make it untenable. These consequences can be personal, like losing relationships, jobs, homes, or communities, or can be severe, like losing one's freedom for behavior that leads to prison.

Often, I will get anger management referrals, some court-ordered, where the individual will come in, somewhat confused, saying, "I've been this way all my life. Either I take mine or someone else will." It is not until they realize the gravity of their consequences that they will reconsider how their hostility bias fuels their potential for violence.

That is where the good news comes in. All four of the components of the hostility bias are very responsive to change, and there are many exercises that can be used to expand their cognitive flexibility and counteract this dysfunctional cognitive set. We can teach people to consider the reality that accidents happen and not everyone is out to get them. We can teach them how to list *many* possible explanations for a situation to have evolved the way it has and come up with many different ways to handle it. And, we can teach people that violence is *always* the *absolutely* last option.

When it comes to violence, people can get hurt...including the person we are working with. There is always someone bigger or stronger or more influential. You may wind up hurting yourself more than the other person if it becomes physical. This can take the form of criminal involvement (being arrested or sued for damages), social isolation, and difficulties in maintaining relationships. In all honesty, a lot of the anger management work that we do is helping people realize other ways, more effective ways, to deal with their emotions—because it is in *their* best interest, not because I can make them change.

Let me offer one last thing about language before we move on. Specifically about cursing. Remember, though, this is a book about psychology, not about etiquette. We live in a very precious society these days, where people have a great dislike for expletives. I am not saying that a gratuitous f-bomb is the answer to all things. In fact, I am partial to those that are particularly well-timed or well-placed. Regardless, it's important for us to understand that people often feel very misunderstood.

They often have difficulty finding the right words to say what they're struggling with, and truth be told, expressing oneself can relieve the pressure of the coiled spring about to explode. I would much rather someone scream a good "Motherfucker!!!" than punch a wall and break their hand. I would prefer someone say "Go fuck yourself" than punch someone else in the face. Cursing and yelling can be hurtful and are not always the most noble, elegant way of handling conflict, but it is sometimes preferable to physical escalation. And let's be honest: It feels good to unload a stream of profanity in the right situation.

The versatility of "fuck" is a power to behold. Anger also has many different subtypes, subtexts, and circumstances in which it might appear, and not surprisingly, the word *fuck* can very easily go along with all of them. For example, exasperation for having to deal with the same shit over and over again: "Here we fucking go again." Exhaustion? Like you just finished your job and now you have more to do? "Fuck!" Or intimidation; for example, when somebody is giving you a hard time and you are fed up: "Are you fucking kidding me?" "You know what I wanna do right now?"

Also, just as anger often is a result of frustration, it can also be a result of disappointment. Like you really hope that after all your preparation, you're going to nail this presentation, and you don't, and you're pissed off at yourself and your audience for not appreciating the work that you put in.

Perhaps the reason why the word *fuck* is so unacceptable, while simultaneously used so often, is for the same reason. We don't want to admit that we're angry. We deny it; we minimize it. *Fuck* is a great word to help express anger. So, if we're not allowed to be angry, then we're not allowed to use the word *fuck*. And let us not forget the wonderful phrase or question that we sometimes ask. "How many fucks does Adam have to give? Adam has no fucks to give."

What does this mean—that he is no longer angry? He no longer gives a shit, and he is no longer giving a fuck. So if you think about the intimacy between the word *fuck* and anger, you'll realize that they are very close friends. Tired of being bullied? "Leave me the fuck alone." Boss not appreciating you? "Can you throw me a fucking bone here? I'm busting my ass for you." Giving up on a task that you've been working on for five hours and have gotten no progress, like trying to put together a bed frame from IKEA? "Fuck it."

Your boyfriend has been with you for a year and a half, and you found out he's been cheating for months, but he wants you to stay in the relationship with him? "Fuck that!" You've been negotiating a deal with a potential client for the last six months, only to find out that he was only raising your bid in order to get a better deal from someone else? "Go fuck yourself!"

Overwhelmed and defeated? "Fuck me." Another driver slowly drifts in front of your car on the highway, without a blinker or looking to see if you're there? "Fucking moron." The applications are limitless... There is virtually no situation that can't be cleanly summarized with one of *fuck*'s many applications.

But when you think about the power of fists versus words, bear this in mind, always and forever: People often feel compelled to respond to language when they actually don't have to, at all. Sure, if someone physically attacks you, you need to defend yourself, neutralize the threat, and remove yourself from further assault (though not necessarily in that order). But if someone says something you don't like, you do not have to respond at all. You can just do...nothing.

This is one of the simplest yet most underutilized tools I coach people on: the hold button. Every phone has one, and humans do too. When things are getting heated or you realize that, for whatever reason, you're too pissed to make a good decision or are about to lose your shit, tell them you're getting another call and you have to go. You basically just put the whole problem on hold. Use the skills you have (or will develop) to adjust the flame of your anger, and come back renewed and ready to negotiate.

This idea—taking a big step back from a problem—is the same thing as a sudden need for a bathroom break. Separate, rebalance, re-engage. You won't regret it, and your brain will be your ally instead of your mouth being your enemy. We think we have to be immediately responsive, and that's just not true. We can, in fact, control the timing of things much more than we think, and when we do, we maintain control over the situation and ourselves more than if we feel constant pressure to be relentlessly responsive.

Ultimately, if people can provoke you, push your buttons, get you angry, they can control you. We see it in sports with trash-talking. We see it in arguments in romantic relationships. We see it in negotiations and in the courtroom with attorneys trying to goad witnesses and litigants. There is a time and a place for cursing. Ultimately, though, whether it is how people talk to you, act toward you, or manipulate you, my hope is that you become like Teflon. Let nearly everything roll off, allowing virtually nothing to stick to you. Allow the things that stick to be worth it, which means: don't waste energy, emotion, or life being easily provoked. It's just not worth it, and it can be really costly emotionally or materially.

5

ADJUSTING THE FLAME

There are few things that bring me greater pleasure than a well-cooked steak. I like mine rare. Charred and sizzling on the outside, cool and juicy on the inside. Do you know the secret to cooking a good steak? Heat. *High* heat. But what happens if you can't adjust the flame, or you leave it under high heat for too long? You wind up with a piece of leather. Forget porterhouse; you might as well go to the sporting goods store and buy a baseball glove, given how tough and tasteless the result would be.

Anger is like fire

 Turn the flame up, it gets hot, cook that steak - good stuff!

 What if you can't turn the flame down? You burn the steak. Now it is like a leather baseball mitt. You burn the steak and you can burn everyone around you.

Anger isn't the problem. It can help you do
great things. If you can't adjust the flame,
you won't reach your goals.

#AdjustTheFlame

Anger is that flame. We know that at moderate levels, anger can make you faster and stronger, have more stamina, and decrease your perception of pain. Anger *helps* performance. Which is why we should and *can* learn to utilize anger. It is like having a nuclear reactor in your belly that can push you to do things that otherwise may be impossible. When we have a coach who rode us too hard, or a teacher who doubted our abilities, we can use the anger connected to that hurt to push us to a *"fuck you; watch me"* energy level that can surpass previous motivation levels. People who don't learn how to master their anger and focus it are leaving money on the table.

But, so many people don't get close enough to the fire to understand it, so they can't adjust the flame and learn to moderate how to use fire to grow and improve themselves. Why?

Because they're afraid, and justifiably so. Because at high levels, anger interferes with fine motor coordination, cognitive processing speed, decision-making, and even vision. When I say vision, I don't mean that you suddenly need prescription glasses. Vision, in this context, is the ability to see, take in, and process sensory data and make quick decisions to create a better outcome. It's like the running back heading to the outside, realizing that the defenders are closing in, and cutting back to a hole in a different gap of the offensive line. It's like the executive who realizes allies who were committing to a joint venture are actually aligning against her, so she pivots to a contingency plan.

Very high levels of anger interfere with these processes—the kind of strategic thinking we require all the time, like having a strategic thinking app always calculating in the background, so we're thinking about the long game instead of being impulsive.

This happens because there is a curvilinear relationship, as described by the Yerkes-Dodson Law, between anger and performance. At very low levels of arousal, most people don't do their best work, like when you first wake up, hence why Starbucks and Dunkin' are billion-dollar businesses. As anger increases, it helps performance, but only up until a point. Then, it crashes. Our goal is to get up to that red line, without going over it.

There is a Zone of Optimal Functioning where performance tends to be best, at moderate levels. Too low, and performance is not great. Too high, and performance tanks. The sweet spot is in the middle. However, it should also be remembered that there are some tasks that higher emotion levels are more advantageous for, and there are skills that require more precision, not to mention some people perform better or worse at higher levels of anger.

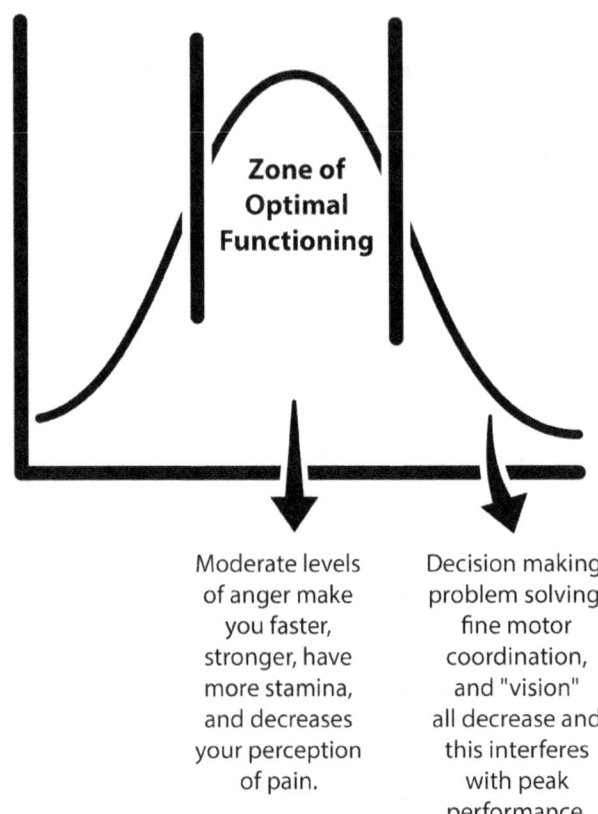

Zone of
Optimal
Functioning

Moderate levels of anger make you faster, stronger, have more stamina, and decreases your perception of pain.

Decision making, problem solving, fine motor coordination, and "vision" all decrease and this interferes with peak performance.

Considering the model above, one also has to understand that there are individual differences between people in how they experience anger and how it impacts their performance, and there are also differences depending upon the task at hand.

Keep in mind throughout these discussions that when I describe arousal, I mean emotional arousal, which can take the form of anxiety or anger. In fact, anger and anxiety are nearly physiologically identical. That's why anxiety interventions often work for anger as well, and fear can flip to anger, and vice versa.

This is too important to walk past quickly. Does this mean that anger and anxiety are opposites? Can they occupy the same place? Originally, psychologists thought, "No. With reciprocal inhibition, two competing emotions cannot occupy the same place." But this is not true. Many emotions can occupy the same place, and at times, they are different manifestations of the same issue. Where anxious people tend to avoid and angry people tend to attack, anxious people may become angry that the world has them by the balls, and they don't live as freely as they'd like.

And though one could (and I have) suggest that they get angry and do something about their unnecessary worry, it does not always work. Because they have ruminated about worrying for so long that they cannot simply "anger it away." They may get pissed in the moment, but they return to their pathological cycle of worry. Thus, people with anxiety issues, even though some of that may be anger turned inward (similar to how depression is sometimes anger turned inward), must address the cognitive components of irrational fear *while* implementing many of the same emotion-regulation skills that we'll talk about later for anger management.

Some people are very sensitive emotionally and quickly escalate from zero to sixty, so when they start getting angry, they quickly go over the red line and become irrational. When this happens, their performance tanks. Others have a very high threshold for tolerating anger and can continue to function well, even at higher levels of anger. That is not to say they're impervious to anger's impact on their capabilities. We're all vulnerable at some level, but their brains can continue to function at higher anger levels than others. These people may even enjoy provoking others around them, knowing that when things get "hot," others may start to falter, while they continue to swim happily in the simmering, boiling water.

In the same light, some behaviors lend themselves to benefiting from higher levels of anger than others. Golf provides a good example of this. When driving from the tee, higher levels of anger may be helpful in driving the ball greater distances. However, while putting, higher anger levels will interfere with the mental planning (considering distance, pitch of the green, how smooth the ball rolls on this course, etc.) and fine motor coordination necessary to execute the perfect putt.

We can see this applied to other situations as well. The mother who can lift a car off of her child can do so because of the extreme strength that the adrenaline rush of fear and protective instincts can provide. When weight training, I used to be able to lift significantly more than my peers because I could summon imagery that would infuriate me. I would convince myself that a given lift would have some impact on the safety of my loved ones, or have the ability to undo some terrible thing that had happened in my life. I would deliberately create cognitive distortions to stimulate that anger that gave me more power and strength. Almost foaming at the mouth with rage, I would explode through a lift, as powerlifters are often seen summoning their deepest anger to push them to do what feels impossible. After maxing out the lift, it took me a few minutes to recompose myself, but I could deliberately summon the anger necessary to get things done.

Similarly, many people know that it's difficult to concentrate and get work done when there are many distractions and irritants around. People who work from home will often go to a Starbucks to find a quieter domain to work, or perhaps this writer is wearing noise-canceling headphones while his ten-year-old son is arguing with the television about something. The point is, there are times when higher levels of anger/arousal can help us, and other times when we're better off turning it down.

That is the core of anger management: adjusting the flame to suit the circumstances. I'm not asking people to assume yoga poses in the middle of competition to calm themselves down. I want to help people identify how they're feeling and adjust the flame to the level that will help their performance, no matter what anyone else is doing. We only have control over ourselves, and using this lever of control and reaction leads to better outcomes. Anger itself is not the problem. It's the amount, the volume, the intensity of the anger—and where, when, onto whom, and how it impacts others—that can interfere with life. Let's learn to adjust the flame.

6

INCREASING SELF-AWARENESS & REDEFINING POWER

A book that doesn't provide tools to deal with your problem is not very useful, so let's fill your toolbox.

Before we discuss the skills involved in anger management, it's important that we first remember that even the most violent people are actually violent a very small percentage of the time. And even when your irritability may be increasing in frequency, duration, and intensity, it's still the minority of your existence. This is the case because you already have several skills you use to modulate your emotions, whether you realize it or not, whether you're doing it consciously or unconsciously, or the skills you've used are less effective than they used to be. You have skills, but they can always improve, and there are always more tools for the toolbox.

One of the more humbling experiences in my career happened in my first year of graduate school when a high school basketball coach asked me to teach relaxation skills to a point guard whose free-throw shooting was deteriorating. I met with Duane and taught him imagery and visualization, diaphragmatic breathing—which slows down breathing and heart rate, decreasing muscle tension, sweating, and shakiness. I also taught him progressive muscle relaxation (PMR) so that he would have tools to help him ground himself, lower his anxiety, and be more successful from the line. He learned the skills easily; however, his poor free-throw shooting got even worse. I was sure that this was a sign that I would have a short career. One of the first athletes I worked with, and I made him worse. Fantastic!

The following week, the coach reached out to me and told me I was off the hook. Not sure what that meant exactly, he explained that while watching Duane, he thought the problem was more technical, and he sent him to a shooting coach, who noticed a problem with Duane's follow-through. He was short-arming his shot, so it was less fluid and repeatable. On the one hand, it was good to hear that Duane's shooting was on the mend, but I found myself questioning my competence. I had to talk to Duane.

Duane was about sixteen years old and a very well-mannered young man, especially for the neighborhood he had grown up in. I started by congratulating him on identifying the problem with his shooting, which he replied to with a shy, closed-mouth smile, seeming to know what I was going to ask him next. Then I followed with, "Duane, I understand you had problems with your shooting, and I wouldn't have been able to detect or fix that problem, but why do you think you got worse with the work we were doing?"

Delicately, Duane explained, "Hey doc, I loved the things you taught me...and they helped me at home. I was getting to sleep easier and felt less stressed overall, but at the line, I started using what you gave me...and well...it screwed up my routine. I used to go, dribble, dribble, backspin, dribble, backspin, shoot..." "Okay...?," I responded. "Well,

I stopped that, closed my eyes, imagined the shot, rolled my shoulders like you taught me in PMR, and then took my shot. It seemed like a good idea, but it felt mechanical and unusual for me, because I'd changed what I was doing since I first started playing."

That's when it hit me: It was not that the skills I taught Duane didn't work...it was that he threw out things that had been working for him. What a critical lesson to learn.

Always remember that people have skills that they use, many of which work well for them. We can add tools to your toolbox, but don't just throw away what you already have and what works for you. The goal is to give you *more* tools to help you specifically, and, if your toolbox is relatively empty, to give you some things you've never tried before. This is a process of self-improvement, of stepping outside yourself so that you see the components and how they work together, which is hard to do.

Every time I work with someone, I'm not starting off with someone who is worthless or has no skills, tools, or experience to draw from. I'm starting with someone who is not experiencing the success they want as often as they could.

I think we need to appreciate that anger issues are not always about skill deficits. Many things could contribute to chronic anger, as well as having a quick temper. The skills will teach you how to better handle those things. However, you should not presume that this is the only manner to treat anger issues, and there will be times when the skills training alone will be insufficient to change a long-standing pattern of reactive aggression. Each person's situation is different.

As is probably clear now, we are often the last ones to know that we're walking around with a chip on our shoulder. If you're reading this book, it means that someone either told you that you are one of those people, you're looking for ideas to help someone who struggles with anger, or you are starting to become aware that you get pissed sometimes and it's hurting you and the people you care about. This last revelation is not something to dread or be embarrassed about. It is, in fact, the first step to increasing your power, because only once you identify a problem can you then do something about it.

How do we increase self-awareness, then? Must we go into therapy? Do we need to sit in quiet meditation for an hour a day? Do we need to conduct surveys of everyone in our lives to get their opinion on our actions? Well...that would not be self-awareness, would it? It would be other-awareness.

I've often joked that there's no such thing as a self-help book. If it is a self-help book, then I'm writing it to just help myself. If you didn't write the book...it is not self-help. It is "other-help," or more aptly a "learn to help yourself" book. That's what we're striving for. To help *you* become more capable of helping *you* become the best, most effective version of yourself.

It all starts with self-awareness, because paying attention to yourself, how you feel, how you think, and how you perceive others and yourself gives you the roadmap you need. Do you notice how people are responding to you? Do you have an observing ego? Can you reflect on yourself? Do you pay attention to your tone of voice, your word choice, your use of profanity, how fast you're talking, your nonverbal accompaniments to your speech, like your facial expressions? Can you see these things? Admittedly it's difficult because, after all, we're looking outward at the world, and we don't have a mirror constantly offering us our reflection to consider.

I remember the first time I was video-recorded for a media clip. I was appalled. *Do I really look like that and sound like that?* I had a face made for radio, I convinced myself. I was really hard on myself. It's not easy, but by seeking out the feedback, even from ourselves, we can improve our self-awareness, and in turn give ourselves the opportunity to improve.

We have tools that are very basic to monitor our interactions when we get angry. These tools were originally developed as part of Dr. Arnold Goldstein's "Aggression Replacement Training," utilized in Dr. Eva Feindler's anger management programs. I later modified them and utilized the "Hassle Log" when I was developing my anger management programs for athletes. Hassle Logs are printable on index cards, which can be thrown in your back pocket and filled out after a situation aggravates you. They ask the *who, what, where, when, why,* and *how* of your dilemma. By filling them out after the fact, even if you didn't handle the conflict well, you start to pick up details and trends as to the circumstances of your difficulties. If you're in therapy, bringing the hassle logs with specific situations to your sessions provides valuable material for discussion, showing that you're not only paying attention to your experiences but also thinking critically about how to address them.

Name:_____

Date:_____

Mor._____ **Aft.**_____ **Eve.**_____

WHERE WERE YOU?

Class_____   Gym_____

Locker Room____   Outside/On-campus_____

Home_____   Dining_____

Off-campus_____   On the field_____

Other_____

WHAT HAPPENED?

Somebody teased me._____

_____

Somebody took something of mine._____

_____

Somebody told me to do something._____

_____

Somebody was doing something I didn't like.

_____

Somebody started fighting with me._____

_____

I did something wrong._____

_____

Other:_____

_____

WHO WAS THAT SOMEBODY?

Another teammate_____   Teacher_____

Coach_____   Parent_____

Sibling_____   Umpire/Ref_____

Other_____

HASSLE LOG

WHAT DID YOU DO?

Hit back_____	Told Supervising Adult_____
Ran away_____	Walked away calmly _____
Yelled_____	Talked it out_____
Cried_____	Told a peer_____
Ignored_____	Broke something_____
Was restrained_____	
Other:_____	

HOW DID YOU HANDLE YOURSELF?

1	2	3	4	5
poorly	not so well	okay	good	great

HOW ANGRY WERE YOU?

1	2	3	4	5
burning mad	really angry	moderately angry	mildly angry	not angry at all

Of course, filling out an index card doesn't ensure that you'll be an insightful person, but at least it will lead you to look at your role in an interaction, rather than just looking at the other parties'. It's the difference between looking for an external cause of an issue instead of seeing our role in it. We often tend to blame everyone else while not considering our part in it, but as always, just because someone is reacting doesn't mean you have to. Remember, when you have one finger pointing at someone else, the other fingers are usually pointing back at you (meaning that we tend to blame others before blaming ourselves... and we usually have some responsibility in every interaction).

Increasing self-awareness requires courage, time, and effort. Contemplate how people see you. Don't forget that people's view of you is not always a match with who you are. UCLA's Hall of Fame basketball coach John Wooden advised, "Be more concerned with your character than your reputation, because your character is what you really are, while your reputation is merely what others think you are." This is important because your character is what you carry with you all the time, and it should be influenced by what you aspire to be. If you're driven by reputation, you may find yourself doing what others expect of you but you detest. As the saying goes, don't accept criticism from someone you would not go to for advice.

Nonetheless, your reputation will often influence how people interact with you. My reputation in prison, before inmates and staff knew me, was interesting: They thought I was part of administration, or I was part of SID, an officer in the Special Investigations Division, the cops who police the cops. Sometimes, they thought I was a cop from the outside. In any case, it helped me because my reputation— this perception of me—carried authority. It didn't hurt that I carried myself as someone who could handle himself in a physical confrontation, if needed. Sometimes, I was able to get things done because of who people *thought* I was. The point is: Know your reputation, and use it to your advantage.

However, the most ideal situation is when your character and reputation fit hand-in-glove with one another. This isn't very common, and I think most people feel misunderstood exactly *because* of this discrepancy. We rarely (if ever) see ourselves the way others do; they can never know what's really on our minds. Our intentions are known only to us, even when we think it should be obvious.

A willingness to examine what values matter to you is a sign of personal opportunity. Do you demand that people agree with you, even subtly, through your behavior? Do you raise your voice or try to leverage, manipulate, or bully people into seeing things your way? Manipulation is not necessarily a bad thing (and we will explore this more later). The issue is that you must ask yourself, "Does this actually work?"

If so, I'm guessing that people may go along with you in the moment to avoid conflict but dismiss you as an asshole to be avoided behind your back. And if this is the case, it's not what you want. It doesn't last, and it leads to relentless, and chronic, avoidable conflict.

There are many reasons why you're likely hesitant to embark on this journey. Looking at ourselves critically isn't easy, and I applaud anyone willing to take a hard look at themselves. In my professional practice, I often work with people who haven't made the choice themselves; instead, it's being forced on them. This is usually because their anger put them in the crosshairs of the law, the criminal justice system, their partner, their parents, or some other external force that makes them examine their role in conflict.

But an ability to do this kind of self-examination pays dividends far beyond being able to avoid getting arrested, charged, and convicted. It can prevent the slow and steady erosion of who we are, so life's minor conflicts roll off our backs rather than leaving us stooped over and burdened. And when done right, this puts you on the path to being much more effective at impacting your environment.

It's not as simple as you being stubborn and viewing your life as: "Fuck 'em... I've always done things my way... I don't have to change." It's scary to consider how you may have ruined relationships, missed opportunities, and hurt people you care about, like your romantic partners, your siblings, your parents, or maybe even your children. If you hurt other people you care about, you're also hurting yourself. Plus, even if you don't care about whoever you've hurt, harming them means they're less likely to be helpful to you in the future. I'm not advocating for always manipulating people to keep them close, but if you make someone lose face, chances are, you'll never get them and their kindness toward you back.

There's a scene in the movie *Monsters, Inc.* that often reminds me of this. Sully, a large monster particularly good at scaring people, yells because in their world, screams produce energy. However, he befriends a human, a little girl named Boo, whom he is trying to save. They're in a room as he demonstrates his terrifying skills. Moments later, he sees her horrified reaction to his tirade, and for the first time, he realizes the damage he can do. Sully feels horrible about his capacity to make someone else feel bad, especially someone he's grown to care for and wants to protect. A lot of people who emotionally explode with anger have had similar experiences.

Whether you have hurt someone or have even a tinge of worry that you may have, being willing to look at yourself honestly, then putting in the effort to improve these interpersonal skills, isn't a sign of weakness; it's pure strength.

7

THE PHYSIOLOGY OF ANGER: ADJUSTING THE FLAME THROUGH AROUSAL MANAGEMENT TECHNIQUES

Imagine, for a moment, that you are not a sophisticated, evolved human being, but instead you are a cute, fuzzy bunny in the woods. You're just chewing on some grass when a large predator jumps out and clearly plans on making you lunch. You don't have to think of a plan; your nervous system will engage. Specifically, your sympathetic nervous system, which is responsible for physiological activation, will kick in. This reaction is known as the fight-or-flight response.

There is also the possibility that you'll be so alarmed that you will freeze, which is unlikely to lead to survival. More likely, though, you will either run or prepare to fight. It doesn't require contemplation or planning, and you don't even think about what's happening. Your body will take over and do what needs to be done.

Interestingly, both anger and fear are nearly physiologically identical because in both scenarios, your sympathetic nervous system is driving the ship. The difference between anger and fear, though, rests in the *thoughts* and corresponding *behaviors*. When you're afraid, your thought is to escape, and the behavior is to flee—even though it may happen so quickly, you're barely aware of the process. When angry, your thought is to attack, and the behavior is to approach to fight. However, when it comes to how your body reacts, in both situations, the same things happen.

Whether fighting or running, your muscles are going to need to be engaged. They tighten up and start contracting in anticipation of whether you're going to fight or run. Those muscles won't work for long, though, without oxygen. That's why your breathing rate increases. Oxygenated blood won't do you much good unless it gets to the oxygen-starved muscles, so your heart rate and blood pressure also increase. You may feel shaky, as adrenaline, the hormone secreted that drives these physiological changes, surges through your body. You'll start to sweat, unless you are refined, then I guess you would perspire.

In either case, how does sweating help you survive? Three ways: sweating will prevent you from overheating. You cool down as the sweat evaporates from your skin. Sweating assists with thermoregulation, which is necessary for prolonged, intense activity. When you sweat, you become slippery. It makes it a lot harder to catch you or harm you when they can't get a good hold of you. And, you stink! It's a simple rule of nature: If something stinks, you leave it alone. Things that stink can be dangerous, on purpose. I know guys in prison who rarely shower, presuming their body odor would make them a less appetizing target of sexual assault, and they are right.

Oh, and you also probably have the urge to urinate, like, right now...urgently! This helps survival as well, because if you had a full bladder and it were ruptured in combat, that could be a dangerous injury. Not to mention the fact that it's harder to run with a full bladder. Oftentimes, people associate this urge to urinate with being afraid, not angry. We've all heard of people becoming so scared that they peed their pants, but what is another phrase for being angry? Being pissed. Coincidence? I don't think so.

It's hard to argue, considering how well we were made to survive, that God or some higher being wasn't involved in our planning. It just doesn't seem to be dumb luck that built us so efficiently, enabling us to adapt as well as we have. But we are incredibly efficient and adaptive, and anger is no less a part of that than any other reaction we're capable of.

Also, these bodily changes are all or none, which means that if one switches on, they all do, and if one goes off, they all do that too. Not only is this important in understanding and identifying when you're getting angry or scared, but it also holds the key to how to de-escalate.

Of the changes we listed above, which can we change directly? Heart rate? Nope, not directly. Don't believe me? Try to stop your heart right now... You can't. Breathing rate? Yep. Don't believe me? Hold your breath for a few seconds. Muscle tension? Absolutely: make a fist and hold it. Shakiness? No. Sweating? You wish. Entire industries are devoted to managing this involuntary response. Urge to urinate? No. You cannot prevent the urge, but you can choose to urinate.

The point is, if we decrease any of these, then we can reverse the process. We can teach people breath control. We can teach people methods to relax their muscles. There are many ways we can teach people to slow themselves down, but they can only do so if they can *identify* what they are feeling, which is why our epidemic of alexithymia (the inability to name emotions) requires some attention.

For most people, all of this escalation happens in a matter of seconds, giving them little time to mentally catch up to physiological changes. For the rare few who are able to know what sets them off and know how to slow it down, let's have a round of applause. By paying attention to how they feel, what they think, and how they react, they maintain control over themselves. Paying attention to their bodies and noting changes is a good way to identify emotions, with a caveat.

When I'm working with athletes and teaching them how to identify their emotions, I review physiology with them, but one also needs to be reminded that in the middle of exercise, practice, or competition, their bodies are going to naturally become activated. They go on autopilot, as we all do when we allow the body to take over. The primitive part of our brain doesn't understand that we are playing a game. It thinks we're fighting or running for our lives, so again, the sympathetic nervous system kicks in to allow for prolonged activity.

Sports are simulations of survival exercises. Your mind may know it's a game, on some level, but your body responds like it's a battle.

So, how can we use our body's activation signals as signs of different emotions if it's already activated as a result of the demands of a game or competition? It's very hard. It means playing on several levels simultaneously, building awareness of not only where the ball, goal, finish line, or teammates are, but where a player is in his or her emotions.

That's why I teach athletes to use two other strategies. First, don't rely only on your *physiological changes* to cue you to anger when competing. Instead, look for a change in your *thoughts*. If you're more focused on executing your opponent than executing the next called play, you have a cognitive shift that is consistent with anger, and it's a sign to adjust the flame. Second, you may be the last to know that you have gone over the line and are now too angry to perform at your best. That's why, especially in team sports, we try to create a culture of shared emotional intelligence, where everyone is responsible for one another.

The coaches and players are collectively responsible for keeping an eye on each other's level of anger and emotional temperature. If everyone is on board—and I've had teams sign a pledge to commit to this plan—then each player will be receptive to feedback, and if they're getting too hot, they agree to take a breather, recompose themselves, and get back into action. Some sports lend themselves to this better than others due to substitution rules, but it creates a culture of composure.

I tell the athletes I work with: Be intense, but when you're over the top, you need to take a moment to chill. Knowing when to step out isn't being penalized, but instead it means being able to perform better, which can mean the difference between not only winning and losing, but losing your shit in destructive ways. It can and often does improve the process. And the better you get at adjusting the flame, the less often you need to be removed from play. Also, it's a reminder that the outcome of a game is not the only variable. Sometimes, your process will be great, and you'll still lose. But if your process is good, you'll win more often in many different ways.

The ultimate goal of teaching an individual the physiology of anger is to support the normalization of and ability to control the flame; that we're hardwired and pre-programmed to get angry. And once again: there's nothing wrong with the emotion, which is hardwired into us. Anger, along with fear, helps us survive. It also gives us a roadmap as to how to reduce the emotions so that we can get to our zone of optimal functioning.

Before you picked up this book, you had tools in your toolbox. Just as in the story of Duane (from earlier in the book), where I inadvertently displaced his relaxation tools with new ones, it's important to always remember that you already possess de-escalation techniques, even if you had no idea you came loaded with this software. Some work well. Some used to, but not anymore. And, there will be some that you develop entirely on your own, as you think about what sets you off, what calms you down, and what makes you feel good.

I can't list every possible skill under the sun, because there are always going to be ways of talking to yourself that are specific to you, and only you. We'll review skills I've used with many different kinds of people to adjust their moods that have been received, implemented nicely, and, most importantly, *work*. This doesn't mean that if you do something you don't read in this book that it's wrong. I challenge you to make sure there aren't any unintended consequences associated with the technique. But, if it works for you and there are no negative side effects, use it.

If you de-escalate by punching walls instead of people, that's catharsis. You'll feel better by expressing the anger outward, but you're also more likely to punch the next time you're angry because the punching was reinforced by feeling better afterward. If you do shots of tequila to calm down, as self-medication, this might work in the short run, but it also might disinhibit you and make you more likely to strike out. If you excuse yourself to calm your breathing, or collect your thoughts, or repeat your most calming and peaceful mantras, then we're in the realm of controlling the flame.

If you reinforce a dangerous behavior while de-escalating, it's clearly not a good choice. Consider what works for you, but try to add to your toolbox, since there are many additional things you may not be aware of until you really focus on what makes you feel better.

Interestingly, when I say adjust the flame, it implies that you might need to turn it up *or* turn it down. This is true because the flame goes both ways. For people who struggle with depression, motivational challenges, or low self-esteem, it may be difficult to motivate themselves, and their flame may be at a permanent, slight flicker, in which it produces barely a degree of heat.

I believe that finding one's anger can be an effective way of defeating depression and anxiety because *some* anger can activate us. But that's another book, because this one focuses on dealing with anger that's too pronounced. When adjusting the flame, I'm referencing turning it *down*—de-escalation techniques—because for people who experience anger intensely or often, this is the part of the equation that needs assistance.

BREATHING

As we saw in the previous section, of the several physiological changes that occur with sympathetic nervous system activation, the two bodily changes that you can control directly are breathing rate and muscle tension. We will start with these because they are at the core of our being, as they are connected to our physiology.

When you ask someone to calm down and take some deep breaths, strangely, they usually don't know how to breathe. Breathing is something automatic. It's something that we don't often concentrate on, and when we do, we tend to trip over ourselves. Because of this, when we do concentrate on it and hijack the autonomic nervous system, we usually screw it up. We don't rhythmically slow our breathing down. We huff and puff, raising our shoulders to our ears, exhaling with great volume. This doesn't help. In fact, it creates new levels of tension. To slow our breathing, we need two things: proper technique and rhythmicity.

Diaphragmatic breathing—in which we consciously take slow, deep breaths using the diaphragm and abdominal muscles—is utilized to instruct and maximize proper breathing technique. When taking a deep breath, your shoulders should remain stationary, because it's your diaphragm (the band of muscles below your ribcage) that should pull down and out. This maximizes your chest cavity and lung space so as to increase both air volume and oxygenation. The easiest way to know if you're doing this correctly is to put your hand on your belly before you take a deep breath. Inhale slowly and fully through your nose (unless you have sinus problems that make this more difficult...in that case, mouth breathing is acceptable), and as your diaphragm pulls down and your chest cavity expands, your belly will push out as if you have a balloon expanding inside you. As the balloon expands and your hand is pushed out slowly, you know that you're breathing correctly.

Ideally, you breathe in through your nose slowly and exhale through pursed lips, meaning that your lips are slightly closed as you push the air out. By exhaling through pursed lips, you create negative pressure in your airways, which keeps them open and increases oxygen exchange throughout the breathing process. As silly as this may feel, it works. Your brain tells your lungs what to do, and allowing your stomach to expand means you're maximizing the available space. When you're doing it right, your hand should come down and out as your diaphragm pulls out.

You also want to create rhythmicity, which means you are breathing in a steady pattern. This pattern can slow down accelerated breathing when you're aroused, meaning that your system is activated and you head into fight or flight. Inhale slowly for a count of four through your nose, hold it for a second or two, and then slowly exhale through pursed lips for a count of six. It may be a little uncomfortable to use this ratio when you first start concentrating on your breathing, or when you're irritated, but the plan is to get to this ratio over a couple of cycles. With the exhalation being longer than the inhalation, your parasympathetic nervous system becomes engaged and contributes to slowing you down overall.

Think of it like this: Your sympathetic nervous system turns everything on, and your parasympathetic nervous system turns it all off. They're both part of the autonomic nervous system, which is automatic, but we can get the system going one way or the other, because they're all in or all out. When you slow your breathing, everything else slows down too.

If this feels weird or unusual to you, don't worry. You've been breathing since birth, and I'm not saying you're doing it wrong, but chances are, you think more about your hair than your breathing. When you start to focus on this part of your physiology and try to control it, it won't feel natural. Expect this, and just practice. Because breathing is at the heart of nearly every relaxation exercise you can do, it's important that you get to know how to breathe correctly, quickly, and easily. It can make you feel better. There's a lot of variability in how people learn this, and some people get this quickly while others struggle with weeks of practice. Whatever your pace, it's normal. Don't sweat it.

There are many apps that are now available to teach breathing exercises. Feel free to go check them out. Breathe2Relax, Breathwrk, CALM, and Headspace are a few that are often used by clients of mine.

In meditation techniques, you may have your attention drawn to your breathing, or some other imagery, to distract you from the problems that stress you. I would recommend, when learning how to breathe correctly, being mindful of it. Practice these skills in bed at night, as they are particularly useful to help you relax and get to sleep. Since it takes a little practice, there's no better time than when you're relaxing and trying to slow your mind down.

Before moving to the imagery components, just close your eyes, with your hand on your belly, and slowly breathe in the cool air, feeling it pass through your nose, down your windpipe, and into your lungs. Feel the muscles of your upper torso accommodate the expansion of your chest. Let your lungs feel full, but not stressed. Hold the breath for a second or so, and then feel the warm, stale air exit your lungs, up through your mouth, and leave your body through pursed lips for a longer count. Pay attention to your senses. What do you hear? What do you feel? Smell? Taste? The more you become aware of your sensory experience, the better you are preparing your mind to pair these breathing exercises with imagery exercises.

Let this process take time. Learn to walk before you run. Don't become frustrated with yourself if you feel no immediate change. People learn skills at different rates. You may feel proficient with diaphragmatic breathing after a couple of trials, or it may take weeks to feel like you have mastered this. Do not worry. That will only contribute to the stressful cycle. Allow yourself to learn these skills correctly, rather than quickly.

Keep in mind that one of the problems with anger management is that when you are losing your shit regularly and then become better at preventing these explosions, people usually don't notice them because they don't see what *doesn't* happen. It is a major frustration when you decrease the times that you are escalating and people don't acknowledge it. But, you know. And you can take pride in your progress.

PROGRESSIVE MUSCLE RELAXATION (PMR)

When we consider how our body responds to a threat, one of the sympathetic nervous system responses is muscle tension. And because the SNS (Sympathetic Nervous System) responds in an all-or-none fashion, just like when we slow our breathing, we can slow our whole reaction. Similarly, if we can reverse our muscle tension, we can also de-escalate ourselves physiologically.

PMR was first developed by Dr. Edmund Jacobson back in 1938 as a method of relaxation, and it attends to the systematic process of contracting muscle groups intentionally and for a prolonged period to heighten relaxation. Similar to how it was discovered in plyometrics (jump training to improve explosiveness)—that if you stretch a muscle before you contract it, it increases the power of the contraction—it is also true that if you hold the tensed muscle for a bit longer, you increase the sense of relaxation afterward.

Like many mental skills, PMR is not something that is a "one and done." It takes significant practice to become proficient. When I am teaching it to clients, I encourage them to practice at least three to five times per week for the first week or two to shorten the learning curve.

I also tell them to pay attention to where their body uniquely houses their stress: the muscle group that is tight most often when stressed. It is not the same for each person. For me, it is my traps (the trapezius muscles that attach my neck to my shoulders). When I'm having a tough day, I often notice that I'm sitting at my desk with my shoulders practically touching my ears. I also note that I am more muscularly fatigued overall. I have learned that if I "roll" my shoulders in a contraction and then relax, I can feel a nice electric chill traveling down my body, and I am more relaxed afterward.

There is no "right" muscle group. For some, it may be their facial muscles from clenching their teeth all day. Or their forehead from their furrowed brow. It may be their calves that are tight. Whatever muscle group it is, pay attention when you are scanning your body as you are learning PMR, because that will be the "sweet spot" that you can use to "adjust the flame" quickly. Remember, for anger management, we are not looking for sedation. We are just looking to decrease the tension enough that we drop below the red line and re-engage our brains in our problem-solving process.

Further, even when you're proficient at it, on some days you might be uncharacteristically grumpy and irritable. PMR may not do it alone. You may need to engage other tools. This is *not* a failure. It is just the reality that some days suck more than others. If you have a full toolkit, you have options. If all you have is a bottle of Jack Daniel's, get ready for liver problems. Have options!!!

Just like breathing exercises, and as you will see with imagery and visualization shortly, even when I offer a script, it is very difficult to actually learn the skill by reading. That is why I am including audio files of a PMR training script. It is much easier to learn by hearing my explanation of the process step by step. It's actually even easier when you see me do the individual muscle contractions. First, it reduces the discomfort of realizing how ridiculous we look during some of the contractions when you get to see me appear silly first. Reducing stigma always helps. But, the other thing is that this feels unnatural at times, and so being coached as you do this is helpful.

Nonetheless, use the audio files as well.

This is *guided* imagery, meaning, I am providing a template for you but you are to individualize it. Though you are being taught how to step through the process, it is your imagery that matters, including the details you insert to make it most vivid. PMR doesn't work that way. You need to follow the script to learn it the way it is presented. But, my script is not the only one out there. You can certainly find other PMR scripts on the web. If you find that another person's voice is more engaging or helpful for you to "get it," that's fine.

Below is a script that I have used and adjusted over the years. Remember: Pay attention to what muscle groups are tightest when you are learning this, as those will be the keys to accelerating the relaxation process.

Okay, are you ready? Now, I want you to get yourself comfortable in your chair. Sit with good posture but without being stiff. Place your back against the chair, let your arms hang loosely at your sides, and place your feet on the floor in front of you. Now, prepare yourself for this exercise by beginning with your breathing. Breathe in through your nose nice and slow, hold it for a couple of seconds, and then slowly exhale through your mouth, taking a little more time to exhale than to inhale. Nice and easy. In and out. Do this for a couple of cycles. If you like, you can close your eyes during this exercise, but it is not necessary.

Some people benefit from imagining things as they breathe. People might imagine their breathing being in sync with waves coming up on the sand and then returning to the ocean. Take a deep breath in with the water coming up, and then release the stress and tension with the water as it returns to the sea during your exhale. Do this a few times yourself to begin to become comfortable and relaxed. Slow everything down. Nothing else in the world matters at this moment. This is your time, your time to control your body and how it feels. Enjoy the feeling of the tensions of the day washing out of you.

Okay, now we are going to begin going through your muscle groups, deliberately tightening them, noting the tension, and then relaxing them. When you are ready, make tight fists out of both hands. Squeeze hard enough to bring slight discomfort. Feel your fingernails sticking into your palms. Feel the muscles in your forearms slowly shake from the strain, and hold them tight without relenting. Maintaining this tension is important for learning about your control over your muscles. Study how your arms feel at this moment. Hold the tension for a slow count from ten.

Begin...ten...nine...eight...seven...six...five...four...three...two. When you reach one, release your fists slowly and let your hands fall gently back to your sides. Pay attention to the warmth coming over your hands. You may even experience a slight tingling and a cooling sensation, perhaps noticing that your hands are cooling off as the blood flows out and the perspiration in your palms starts to dry. Your hands may feel heavy. I want you to notice the difference between the tension you felt a moment ago and the relaxation that you feel now. Continue to breathe slowly and enjoy feeling the difference...the relaxation... You did this...because you are in control.

After breathing slowly and rhythmically for a couple more moments, gently nod your head when you are ready to continue. Good...we will move on. Now, I want you to lift up your arms and bend them at the elbow, bringing your fists toward both sides of your head as you did when you were showing off your biceps as a kid. Tighten those biceps and at the same time expand your chest and push your elbows farther back like a butterfly slowly moving its wings backward. This movement should create some tension in your upper back as your shoulder blades are pushed together. I want you to focus on the overall tension that you are feeling in your upper body...perhaps in muscles that you do not pay much attention to during the day.

For a lot of people, their upper back is where their stress accumulates and seems to "hang out," weighing them down. Again, hold on to the tension. Welcome it because you control it. You are deliberately summoning it, and you can make it leave whenever you want. You may feel the muscles start to fatigue a little bit. This is good. The relaxation will feel that much better.

As the muscles are swelling up from the blood rushing to the area, I want you to slowly relax your biceps. Let your hands fall toward your lap, but before you focus on those biceps relaxing, raise your shoulders up as if you are trying to touch your ears with them. Feel the tension move up your back from your shoulder blades to those traps, the muscle that connects your neck to your shoulders. Tighten them up. This is another place where a lot of stress accumulates. Push those shoulders up toward your ears and feel the tension. Hold it. I know that the muscles are getting tired; just maintain it for a couple more seconds.

Okay, now slowly roll your shoulders backward and then let them fall relaxed. You may feel a chill go down your back as you do this.

Let your shoulders droop down. Let the blood flow out of them. Notice the difference in the tension. Become familiar with it. Enjoy the relaxation and master it. Center yourself again and refocus on your breathing. Nice and easy.

* * *

After a couple more moments, we are going to move on to your facial muscles. Just keep breathing and notice the tension leaving your body. You should already be feeling more at ease than before, but if not, don't worry. You are learning more about your body, and the more familiar you become with it, the greater control you have. Continue your breathing so it is nice and slow and in a smooth rhythm. Time the waves coming in, inhale slowly for a count of three, and hold it, thinking about the waves breaking on the sand. Then gradually release your breath for a count of five, sending your stress out to an open sea that can hold all of it for you. Pause a moment to scan your body and notice how it is feeling.

* * *

Okay, now are you ready? Whether you realize it or not, your face has many muscles in it, and your emotions tend to spend a good deal of time there. Laugh too long and your cheeks hurt. Angry too long, and your brow is tired at the end of the day. We are going to cleanse your facial muscles from the emotional tension. First, spend a moment exploring those muscles. Open your mouth wide, hold it, and then release it. Next, smile big, real big. Hold it for a moment or two, and then slowly release it. Then I want you to raise your eyebrows up. Raise them high like you are trying to touch the ceiling with them…

hold them up. If you want to, feel the skin on your forehead, which may be wrinkling a little bit with the pressure. Hold it...now slowly bring them back down, but do not relax them.

Bring them all the way down so that your brow is tight, you look angry, and your eyes are squinting. Your eyebrows are practically touching, and your forehead is tightening. At the same time, I want you to tighten your jaw and clench your teeth together as if you are holding on to something. Your jaw is now like a vice. Imagine that as your teeth are tightening and your brow is pulled down that you are trying to make your bottom jaw and your eyebrows somehow meet. This is the face of tension. The face of anger. The face of rage. You can make your face this way. You can control all your muscles in your face and all the tension that you are feeling. Your face is like a contorted knot, and you made it happen because you are in control.

Feel your teeth pressed together. Feel your face becoming tired. Now, when I count down from three to one, slowly relax the muscles in your face: three...two...get ready to relax...one. Good...now release all the pressure from those muscles and let them relax. Refocus on your breathing. It might have increased during this relaxation exercise. It is okay. You can calm it all down. Let your tongue sit comfortably in your mouth. Your jaw is no longer clenched, and the strain in your muscles just drops down from the top of your skull and out the bottom of your jaw. Just let it all go. Excellent. Enjoy this for a moment or two...just breathe and relax.

As you continue breathing, we are going to use this steady process as a way to experience tension as well. Breathe slowly, in and out. Now I want you to take in a very deep breath and hold it. Notice the discomfort and the muscles in your expanded chest. Hold on just a little longer, not to the point that you get dizzy. If you get dizzy, stop the process and restore your breathing. But, if you can, hold it so that you can feel that your body wants to release the heavy, carbon-dioxide-filled air and replenish it with cool, oxygen-rich air. And then... release slowly. Your body will breathe quickly at first. This is normal—don't worry. Help your body regain control of your breathing, slowly and steadily.

Okay, now we'll go down the torso to the abdomen. Although these muscles do not usually hold a great deal of our stress, we want to experience the difference between tension and relaxation in all parts of the body. Slowly, I want you to pull your abdomen in as you did when you were young and tried to show everyone how skinny you were. Suck it all the way in toward your spine. Hold it for a moment, but not too long because breathing in this position is next to impossible. But hold it long enough to feel the strain on the muscles. Now slowly relax with an exhale and return your breathing to a slow, steady rhythm.

Continue down to the lower abdomen. We will now tense and then release those muscles, along with the muscles of your hips and upper thighs. Remember to continue breathing between the exercises. It's about balance and rhythm. Now, I want you to place your hands on the sides of your chair for support and then squeeze your knees together as if a balloon is between your legs. Then pull your legs up toward your chest. You will feel tension in your hips and lower abdomen, as well as in the muscles on the inside of your thighs. You may not be accustomed to focusing on them, so they may tire quickly. If they do, hold it for as long as you can. If they do not tire, hold it until you feel the burn. Then, like before, slowly relax and place your feet back on the floor, paying attention to the sensation of relaxation.

Notice how heavy your legs felt while you held them up, and now how nice it feels for them to be supported by the floor. Continue breathing. Relax.

Now we will move on to your legs. We are going to tighten up your thighs and calves now. If you have any problems with your knees, be careful with this one. If it causes pain, just do the exercise with as much extension as you can until it hurts. When you are ready, lift your lower legs up so that your legs are straight, as they are when you are doing leg extensions in the gym. You should feel your thighs tighten, and you may be able to feel the cuts in the muscles of your legs as they contract. Enjoy that tension. Feel the blood filling the muscles while you continue to breathe nice and slow. Keeping your legs straight; point your toes out straight ahead. Think about a diver in pike position or a gymnast pointing their toes in mid-flight.

While holding your toes as straight as an arrow, push your feet downward and feel the tension building at the bottom of your calf. Hold it for a couple of moments. Notice the tension, and notice the difference from relaxation. Hold it a little longer. Okay, now slowly let your feet find the floor and pay attention to the relaxation that you feel throughout your body. Notice and appreciate the control, the power, that you have over your body. Nobody makes you tense. Only you do, and you can stop it. You are learning how.

We'll move on to the last muscle group now. Your muscles may be getting tired. This is good. They cannot be tense and tired at the same time. Enjoy the exhaustion. You made it happen. It's the same as a good workout. You work the muscles and then they relax after being used, but they become tired.

Okay, now place your heels on the floor and raise your feet up on an angle. Try pulling them toward you. You're not using your hands, just the muscles in your ankles and legs. Point your feet up to the sky. Feel the tension in your lower shin. Pay attention to the tension spreading through your feet. Again, enjoy the tension. After holding for ten to fifteen seconds, let it go. Then relax. You are feeling great and doing a great job.

Now, before we finish, scan your body from head to toe. Go through the muscle groups one by one. What is still tense? Anything? If so, repeat or just remember that this place might need more work. You are going to practice this every day, maybe more than once a day, until you become really good at it. Then you will be able to do a quick body scan and relax the culprit, the muscles where the tension is. Eventually, you'll be able to relax everything by just hitting the target muscles. You can do this. You did a great job.

IMAGERY & VISUALIZATION

Imagery and visualization represent the collective actions of conjuring up scenes in your mind for a specific purpose. The purpose for us, at this time, is for relaxation; however, it's also an opportunity for self-improvement, which we will touch on a little later.

A cautionary note, however, before going down the imagery and visualization path: Some people have had traumatic pasts that are prone to intrusive thoughts, flashbacks, and dissociation. Imagery exercises can take them back to a bad place, one where they feel like they are reliving the horrible events of the past in real time. They may dissociate, disconnect from what is going on in reality, and they may even start having emotional reactions to things that they don't see or know about. In extremes, this can include them flailing and fighting off attackers who are not really there. It can be terrifying and dangerous to them and those they're close to. So, if you have trauma in your history, tread lightly. If you are encouraging someone to use imagery and visualization skills, be mindful that there are risks.

I recently provided a masterclass on trauma to sport psychologists and students, and I raised this caution. A colleague offered a specific question that I will now include in my process: "Are you aware of any particular things that we may want to avoid in an imagery exercise?"

This was an important question. I had an athlete whom I was starting to teach imagery exercises to years ago, and I started with a beach scene to elicit relaxation, only to find out the hard way that she had been sexually assaulted on a beach years prior. We were able to recognize it quickly, likely because of my experience with trauma, but to the untrained eye, it could have been messy. So, when it comes to walking around inside someone's head, whether it's yours or someone else's, make sure you get permission to do so, and be aware that though this may seem like a benign activity, there are times when it could be more precarious than you might realize.

Research has shown that people have great variability in their perspectives and ability to learn and utilize imagery skills. Some people have been doing this all of their lives, already in possession of a rich visual inner monologue. Some people pick it up right away, and others struggle to conjure up anything in their minds. Fortunately, the last group is relatively rare. However, if you find learning these skills really challenging, don't worry. We will discuss so many different relaxation and arousal management techniques; some combination is likely to feel right for you.

Perspectives vary. Some people conjure up images through their own perspective or visual viewpoint, which we call first person, like they're seeing it through their own eyes. Others tend to create images of themselves observing themselves, which we call third person. Some research shows that people report greater subjective experiences of "reliving" when they picture events from first person, as opposed to the third-person perspective. My experience has been that when learning imagery and visualization, especially for relaxation, the first-person perspective works best, so that is what I will recommend. However, please keep in mind that, with all of these things, there are many roads to Rome.

Also, visualization experiences tend to be more vivid, and thus more powerful and effective, when they are more sensory. So, pay attention to what each sense is contributing: what you see, what you feel, what you hear, etc. And, because the sense of smell bypasses the thalamus and goes directly to your brain, it tends to have the most robust relationship with memory. That is why if you are trying to recall memories (both good and bad) and you try to recall the smells that you experienced, it can bring the memory better into focus. I know that when I inhale that very specific salty air near where the waves are crashing into a foam, it brings me to a happy, nostalgic place. Think about the smells that bring you back to your relaxing memories.

Moreover, imagery can enhance what you're already starting with breathing exercises, especially when we incorporate visualizations of nature. I will provide a script for beach scene imagery and relaxation shortly, but let's also examine the reasons why nature is so soothing, versus imagining Times Square on New Year's Eve.

Imagine for a second that you're standing next to the ocean and watching the waves come in and go back out to sea. This is rhythmic and reliable. It's also easy to remember the power of the waves. These waves have been hitting the shore around the clock—twenty-four hours per day, 365 days a year, since before humanity existed. Could you imagine it was your job to make sure this was going on? Nature reminds us how vast and powerful it is, and, by comparison, that we are small. Yes, this can bring on feelings of insignificance, but more importantly, it gives us a sense of an often helpful perspective.

If we are small, then by comparison, so are our problems. When we put problems in perspective, they are easier to face and solve. Regardless of whatever drama we're facing, there is something bigger. Bluntly, Mother Nature continues to do her thing regardless of the shit we're stressing over. It's up to us to put our problems in proper perspective, roll up our sleeves, and handle our business. And *breathe*. In order to do that, we need to find the best version of ourselves. We need to practice imagery and visualization, like any skill, to grow proficiency.

When I'm teaching my clients this, I recommend they try to go through the scripts at least three times per week, preferably every night, before they get ready to go to sleep. When done right, the relaxation can slow your mind and resolve tendencies toward insomnia.

Try the following meditation (which I also have available in an audio version if you'd like) when you feel your shoulders rise and your blood pound in your head. And before you roll your eyes, trust me. It works.

* * *

Okay.
Are you ready?

Are you comfortable in your chair? Just sit comfortably with your feet on the floor and your hands relaxed in your lap or at your side.

Start by taking a couple of deep breaths, as we've discussed in the past, in through your nose. Hold it, then exhale through your mouth. Nice and slow.

Gently think about how you are feeling and slow yourself down so that you are getting ready to begin.

Now, I want you to remember that I will be guiding you. But this is your world, and you're free to change the things to whatever makes it most real and most relaxing.

We're going to go to the beach now. Let's begin by tying your breathing to the waves to keep you grounded and in a good rhythm. Time your breathing with the waves as a wave comes in. Take a slow, full breath, blowing up the balloon in your stomach.

Hold it while the white foam rolls up on the sand, and then release it as the water goes out. Take any stress you have with it. Remember how big the ocean is. It can hold all of your problems. Your problems are small compared to the ocean.

Think about all of the different things that your body is experiencing. Can you hear the wave gently crashing on the sand? Perhaps you can see the water coming up toward your feet. Think about the temperature of the air. Is it hot? Is it cool? What season is it? What time of the day is it?

But you are alone. This is your time. Your scene. And you can create it any way you want. Remember that you want this to be comfortable.

Maybe you can feel the sun warming your skin. Maybe you can feel a cool breeze moving the hairs on your arm.

Maybe you see the light from the sun coming through your closed eyelids.

Imagine that you are looking up at the sky and feeling the sun land squarely on your face. Notice every detail. Pay attention to what your senses are telling you.

Notice subtleties in the way you feel, maybe cooling little beads of sweat on your forehead. Pay attention to how your body feels.

Maybe you feel the sand under your feet, and you dig your toes in, and you can feel the coarseness. And as you dig your toes in, the sand is a little bit moister and cooler.

Pay attention to all of the senses. Maybe you see a jetty off to the side. Maybe you see birds sitting on it and squawking, or maybe a seagull diving into the ocean.

Maybe you smell the salt in the air. There is a calmness. There is nothing that you have to do right now. Just focus on your breathing and enjoy where you are. You can go here whenever you want.

This is your image. Think about the waves coming in in front of you. Though they crash, they are quiet and calm by the time they reach your toes. Make this your scene.

Focus on all the different things that your body is telling you. But most importantly, remember that you've made this happen, and you can go back to the beach whenever you want. Spend some time looking around. What else is there? What else do you see? What else do you hear? Enjoy this. This is up to you. Now, I want you to scan your body and determine whether or not you feel better now than before you started. If so, realize that you did this, and so you can make it happen again when-ever you want. The key is paying attention to all of your senses. I'm going to step away now, and you can enjoy this scene, your relaxation. And the fact that you can decide how stressed you are or how relaxed you are. You can summon this image whenever you want to guide yourself down and away from your tension.

* * *

Based on my decades of experience and thousands of patients, clients, and teams, I know that this requires emotional balance, and I also know we can achieve it within ourselves. Okay, so let's consider the vastness of the ocean. Do you think if you took all of the sturm and drang—the storm and stress—that you're dealing with, and threw it into the ocean, it would substantially change the ocean? If you put a single drop of food coloring in a wave, would it turn the whole ocean red, or would it quickly become diluted and irrelevant? The latter. It would dissipate so quickly, it would be imperceptible. Please don't get me wrong. I am not invalidating or minimizing what you may have experienced, or what's making you feel so fucking angry. I'm encouraging you to see it as part of the past, and you don't have to carry it around like an anvil tied to your neck.

Now, back to the waves. Let's incorporate that into our imagery. Assimilate your slow diaphragmatic breathing with the rhythm of the waves. Close your eyes and imagine that the cool air entering your lungs is the clean, crisp breeze coming off the ocean, so that your inhalation is timed with the wave approaching the shore. As the wave rolls up to white, aerated foam on the sand, changing the color of the ground beneath it, you're holding your breath for a second, and as you exhale, the wave is taking your stress, your stale air, and all of your burdensome problems with it back into the ocean to be diluted, leaving you feeling lighter and more relaxed.

This imagery works well for many people. The metaphors match the optics. You are literally throwing your problems out at sea, where they'll be pounded into microscopic particles and will be carried away, far from you. However, this is by no means the only option. Consider what scenes soothe you and take yourself there. While the beach scene allows the cycles of breathing to be in sync with the ocean's waves, it need not be the only way to get there.

As I alluded to above, imagery and visualization can provide the backdrop to mastering relaxation exercises; however, they can also offer a valuable training ground. In the sport psychology world, we've long known the power of utilizing one's mind in mental training to provide repetitions imaginally – in one's mind, rather than in one's movements – that prepare for in vivo (in person, in real time) practice and competition. Abundant research shows that the parts of your brain that correspond to different body parts activate on PET scans when you imagine using them. If you're imagining running, the motor cortex of your brain that corresponds to your legs will activate, and imagining your entire nervous system calming and relaxing does something similar. This is evidence of the tight mind-body connection, and why awareness of how the body feels works with how our emotions are firing.

Often, athletes are trained to imagine perfect performance. A golfer, for example, will visualize the whole course. They'll think about the strategy for each hole, planning their work and working their plan. They'll imagine their caddy handing them their directed club, and they'll mindfully attend to each detail as they approach the tee. They'll pay attention to the smell of the grass, how the breeze may feel, and what they see. They'll visualize birds in the trees to the left of the fairway and clouds on the horizon, and they'll feel the air temperature. What they're doing is allowing their mind to free itself, so their muscle memory can take them through their backswing, striking the ball, following through, and watching the ball penetrate the blue sky. They might work on individual skills, like driving or pitching or putting; some might even take the time to play the whole course in their mind. If they can make it happen in their mind's eye, they can make it happen in real time.

I recommend that imagery is also a modality that can be used for problem-solving, to help people learn how to master situations when they're angry. Once a person can create peace in their minds with imagery, and can then conjure up images of their successful efforts on the green, in the boardroom, and in life, they can then use the mind as a training arena for role play, strategy, and reacting to emotionally difficult circumstances, including, or perhaps especially, anger.

In guided imagery exercises, either the therapist will provide the cues or the individual can insert them themselves. The cues would progress from minor annoyances, with the person working their way through them. The individual would notice how much more difficult it is to solve the problems as their anger rises. Admittedly, sometimes it's funny to watch how people will not keep a pulse on their anger. Their anger will escalate, and they will throw a temper tantrum and sabotage their whole plan.

I was working with a corporate ladder-climbing executive who was frustrated with the old-school, boys-network obstacles she faced that her male colleagues didn't. She was imagining a scene in which she was presenting a shift in marketing strategy she had developed, based on new research data she had uncovered.

We rehearsed her scene in the boardroom with "simple" barbs. One of the senior partners showed up ten minutes late and then disrupted the introduction by taking orders for coffee to be ordered. Michelle was able to handle this well because she had already calmed herself internally.

Having already envisioned the experience, she recognized that this was more about her partner's narcissism than her competence, affording her time for a couple of deep breaths. She even smiled, realizing it gave her an opportunity to scan the room after she had already started, taking a moment from "presentation mode" to assess if anyone seemed likely to be a problem for her. By the time the coffee order was completed, her partner recognized the chaos and disruption he had caused, and he was deferent to Michelle, which she realized he might not have been if he hadn't caused this problem. He apologized and complimented her. "I have been really looking forward to your ideas. I am sorry I broke the flow...please proceed."

Michelle proceeded to present the research. While she showed that sales trends of different demographics were changing, she noticed a colleague, Steve, rolling his eyes and nonverbally dismissing her words. He had been at the firm two years longer than she had been. He had been trying to date her secretly and had vacillated between singing her praises and devaluing her, especially in front of higher-ups in the company. Michelle shifted her eye contact toward others who were more engaged, and she recognized that her shoulders were getting tight. She was distracted and, because this was a practice run in an imagery exercise, asked if she could stop...recognizing that she was struggling.

I encouraged her to continue, pointing out that this was only practice in a safe place. She rolled her shoulders, like she had learned in progressive muscle relaxation, and restarted. Finally, just as she was about to restart, I suggested, "Once you start talking, Michelle, imagine that Steve interrupts you. He says the research you are citing is old and flawed, and no changes should be considered based on a weak base of information."

She had already prepared for that, but she was too hot and blew up. While in the imagery, she turned and said, "*You know what, Steve? Shut the fuck up! You have been brown-nosing our executives since before I got here, but when you try coming on to me, you think you're smarter than everyone in this room and that it will only be a matter of time before you take control of the company and wipe out all of the partners. All the while, you think you are better than you are. You slouch. You annoy people. Your breath stinks and is as stale as your ideas...so please, just shut the fuck up...really...shut up...go on your phone and look at the date of the research I am citing. It came out this month...you dick!*"

Before she even opened her eyes, she had a sheepish grin on her face. She turned to me and said, "THAT was fun...but it wouldn't help me..." It was brilliant. While appreciating the pleasure of catharsis, she also kept her brain working and was assessing her actions and plan. Michelle was able to take a moment and go off the rails *imaginally* and predict the consequences of her behavior (another skill we'll work on later) if she went down that path. She recognized that the escalation pushed her beyond her ability to work her plan.

So, while it was funny and momentarily cathartic, Michelle was able to use her visualization as a stadium, a difficult conversation, or a virtual boardroom, where there might be provocations headed her way, impacting her anger level and influencing her ability to effectuate her goals. She planned her game before she got there, priming her brain and her responses, so she was as emotionally and mentally prepared as she could be and able to support herself. I thought it would have been great theater to tell him off that way, even though it wouldn't have helped her, but maybe she'd have another chance someday.

Equally important, as I mentioned at the outset of our skills discussion, is the point that these skills overlap and do not have to be utilized sequentially. When we reviewed what happened in her scene, Michelle was able to identify several of her triggers that she could use to prepare herself to start cooling down, before blowing up at Steve. For her, she realized that her triggers included: being marginalized and sexualized as a woman in a "man's world"; nonverbal cues being more damaging than verbal affronts that everyone hears; her own self-doubt, which leads her to counterpunch when someone challenges her; and that she was sleep-deprived, as she had ruminated about this presentation for most of the night, leading her to be irritable due to being exhausted.

This led to great planning for the next round of imagery trials. But the most important lesson to learn here is that imagery and visualization are not just for relaxing or creating the perfect performance, but an arena for trial and error, including when provoked and angry.

To be fair, no amount of visualization will ever account for the variables introduced by people we have no control over. But in going through this a few times, Michelle found the many places where she was in total control of herself and her reactions, thoughts, feelings, and anger. She saw what might set her off, and she was able to drive around, or even over, these obstacles.

DISTRACTION

For those of you old enough to remember the show *The Honeymooners*, Jackie Gleason's character, Ralph Kramden, advises, when angry, to recite out loud to yourself, "Pins and needles, needles and pins. It's a happy man that grins." Then, put on a big smile and say to yourself, "What am I mad about? And believe me, you won't remember what you're mad about."

Of course, the landlord raising the rent 15 percent immediately challenges Kramden's ability to keep cool. He storms out of the room, furious. When he returns, irate and ready to argue with the landlord, his buddy Norton tries to remind him, "Hey Ralph, pins and needles," and Ralph bellows, "Aww, shut up!" with his eyes bulging.

The beauty of the skit is that it is not so easy to calm yourself, even with a seemingly infallible mantra. Yet, what it was trying to show was that by distracting yourself from what irritates you, you can lower your flame.

This used to play out when I was bouncing in clubs in the city. You'd have two guys ready to go to beat each other up, usually over something stupid and fueled by alcohol. Once squared up, it's a matter of pride, and no one wants to back down, especially if others may be watching. They would lock eyes and become entrenched in what was about to happen. Left alone, they would go after one another, and I and the other bouncers would have to peel them off one another and end their nights.

However, we knew the dance. We'd intervene early and each with the same strategy, break the gaze of the two wannabe gladiators and ask them a simple question, "Why are you paying attention to that asshole when that girl over there is waiting for you?" Almost always, they'd turn to me and ask, "Where...?" Then I'd walk them away from the conflict while my partner was doing some version of the same thing with the other guy. It wasn't foolproof, but it worked a lot.

Why? Because we distracted them and offered something they wanted more than a fight: attention from a woman. Most of the time, these guys were fighting over their bruised egos anyway. They were pulled away and they saved face because they would have fought if security hadn't stopped them. Now everyone had a chance to go back to having a good night. How did we do it? By distracting them.

For this reason alone, mindless TV, scrolling on your phone, or playing video games are good opportunities to take your mind off things that are annoying you. Of course, this can present its own problems as well. A recent presentation I attended informed us that the average American scrolls through three hundred feet of social media per day. That's as high as the Statue of Liberty, we were warned. These distractions can help de-escalate us when we're pissed, but be mindful that left unchecked, these distractions can lead us to waste a whole lot of time and don't actually calm us down. Quite the opposite; they overstimulate us and become addictive, as they were built to do.

Another de-escalation technique to consider is exercise. Very simply, you cannot be physiologically in a rage at the same time that you are exhausted from working out. It is called reciprocal inhibition; opposite physical states can't occupy the same place. My experience tells me that intense, short-burst exercises can be very effective at releasing pent-up anger. Sprinting, whether running or swimming, heavy weightlifting (though be careful not to use weight that is more than you can comfortably handle), or any other explosive exercise, can be helpful in taking the edge off. Just be sure, as I discuss later when exploring the utility of "rage rooms," to avoid striking exercises when angry. When you do that, punching a bag or kicking pads, you will feel better afterward. But then, when angry, you will be more likely to strike...and what happens when you don't have a bag nearby but there's your shitty neighbor? Right. Call an ambulance, or the police, or both.

One note about this, though: Anger is a powerful ally, and if you can summon your anger and harness it, especially when exercising, you'll likely find that you will lift more than you ever have—a great time for a personal-record lift attempt—go faster, and go for longer. It can help you in training...and in competition. However, you have to be able to get up to that red line without going over it, and that takes a lot of practice.

MUSIC

How about some tunes? Is there a relationship between anger and music? Are you fucking kidding me? Who doesn't get amped with the first chords of Journey's "Don't Stop Believing" or Metallica's "Enter Sandman"? There is no doubt that music can excite us, and it can be whatever kind of sound works for you.

In general (and there are exceptions), heavier bass and faster beats per second are going to activate us, especially at high volumes. Many people keep an activating and a relaxing playlist on their phones. And if you don't, do so, because you can use them, and they serve different purposes.

Also, smoother, rounder sounds, at lower volumes, with slower beats per second and less bass, tend to be more relaxing. I would caution you, however, to stay away from ballads. I know...nice mushy music makes you want to turn to Jell-O, right? Not so fast. You see, we're trying to get you to relax. Ballads, by definition, are slower, sentimental, or romantic songs. And they have lyrics. Those lyrics make you think. And sometimes, they make you think of things that might be a bit more activating, like the way this song led to a night of passionate lovemaking, or how it might remind you of your girlfriend who cheated on you. My point is that the words in ballads could take music that would normally soothe the savage beast and potentially amp you up in the wrong direction, so be mindful of that.

To avoid this potential unintended consequence, I recommend music that is relatively lyric-free. I am partial to smooth jazz. Chris Botti in particular. Find what works for you and have the playlist available before you need it.

I cannot emphasize enough that you have to know what works for you specifically. I have seen athletes who listen to quiet, soothing music (one football player listened to classical music) before the storm of football collisions, while others pump glass-shaking power tunes.

Similarly, I know people who have grown up with and become desensitized to *their* music, even loud music that is normally invigorating, so that they chill when they hear it. While most people get ready to pump it up when they hear the first couple beats of Notorious BIG's "Hypnotize," I know people who sit back and just bob their heads slowly to the rhythm with a laid-back smile.

Making playlists is far easier than the old days, when you needed to catch a song playing on the radio and press the record and play buttons at the same time, and then dubbing them with a dual cassette player. Now you can make a playlist in a matter of minutes.

Whether you prefer Spotify, Apple Music, or some other format, have at least two different playlists. The ON and the OFF. The former gets you amped, and the latter chills you out. Over time, you will realize that some songs will stand the test of time and some won't do it for you anymore. I'd recommend reassessing your playlists' impact on your mood every six months or so. If you put your ON list through your speakers before you work out and you're thinking about going back to bed, it's time it gets cut from the list.

JOURNALING

For some people, the idea of writing things down when they feel like punching a wall may seem impossible. And, it may well be. However, there is value in writing, so long as you aren't so angry that you snap the pen in your hand. One thing it does is allow you to cathart—to feel or express your emotions—onto paper without judgment, response by someone who disagrees, or invalidation.

Don't underestimate the value of writing down how you feel, and not only for the release of getting it out that's provided at that moment. Have you ever gone back and read your own personal thoughts later? It can be both jarring and a pleasant relief to learn that you no longer feel the way you did then, that the storm passed, that anxiety lifted, and that the feelings mellowed into something you can live with. It's like lowering the flame over time. It's impossible for things to remain unchanged, and the way you felt in the heat of a difficult time nearly always levels out.

Seeing this change in yourself is important. It allows you to see where you were and where you are now and hopefully see how you've learned improved skills to cope with the things in life that make you angry. You might think, *Oh, I'll remember. I'll never forget the rage and fury of that time.* But you will. It's nearly impossible to remain at that temperature, so seeing your former self can be really informative.

Getting out what irks you can also allow you to recognize themes about what gets your goat. We will talk about triggers shortly, but it's critically important that you start to identify the things that get you going. You might find those ideas, conflicts, themes, or triggers in your writing. Patterns might emerge. The same features of one particularly difficult person or stressful situation or environment might appear, leading you to realize: *Oh, I guess the mall parking lot on a holiday weekend really DOES enrage me. I guess I should avoid massive, stressed-out crowds.* Or: *My neighbor's wretched taste in music is STILL driving me insane. I suppose I'll try a calm conversation instead of beating their door down next time.*

The other thing that you can get from journaling is an opportunity to see how your brain works (or doesn't) when you are furious. We underestimate the fact that our brain simply doesn't work as well when we're angry. By the way, it's one of the reasons we often lose arguments when pissed. By writing things down and going back to review them after the fact, we can identify triggers, insecurities, and how fucking bananas we sometimes get when in a good snit.

8

TRIGGER RECOGNITION

Congratulations! You now have a toolbox to adjust your flame. Now the question is: When are you going to use it? The simplest answer is: The earlier, the better...and much more often. A serious problem for many people is that they don't see the red line until they have already gone over it.

The reason we start with teaching the physiology of anger after normalizing the emotion is that you can recognize the changes in your body as a sign that you are escalating. That can be a cue that you want to go to your toolbox. However, it isn't the only way, and that too is rather late, because the biological anger cycle is already amping up.

What we really want to do is to learn our triggers—the things that pretty reliably piss us off and get us acting like ogres. Some triggers are obvious and are called Direct Triggers. These are the things that most everyone responds to. A punch. A push. A curse. An insult. Direct Triggers are easy for anyone to see. In these situations, the outside observer sees you react and often says, "That other person had it coming. They started it." This is not to say that responding to Direct Triggers is okay, and that you will be exonerated. You probably won't. And that doesn't just mean that you can hire the best lawyer, defend yourself honorably, and emerge the moral victor, after a protracted battle in which you convince a jury of your peers that you had no choice but to defend yourself. Most of the time, events never rise to the level of legal consequences, but instead, there are social, professional, and costly interpersonal bills to pay.

It's more like saying others would *understand* why you reacted the way you did. But you'll still deal with the consequences. Remember, the goal is to be unflappable, regardless of whatever is going on. I am not advocating for anyone to take a beating, physically or verbally, but we have choices on how we respond. It bears repeating because it's so important: Any fight you avoid is another one that you walk away from.

It sounds dramatic, but you never know when a fight will lead to someone winding up dead...or in the hospital...or in jail. Violence should always try to be avoided. If it's unavoidable, be quick and decisive. Strike and create space so that the threat is neutralized and/or you have a greater ability to escape.

What's really important to identify, however, are your Indirect Triggers. These get at your insecurities. Maybe you're aware of them. Maybe you're not. Maybe these are unconscious conflicts you've struggled with all your life but have never told anyone about, except maybe your therapist, if you have one.

They're often connected to our need to be accepted and to be good enough. If you had a childhood in which you were bullied, or your parents were particularly emotionally unavailable or punishing, or your older sister teased you mercilessly...whatever the case, especially when we are young, we're susceptible to people challenging our personal worth. This can deeply damage our sense of self. This sets the stage for us to be prone to teasing, barbing, or provoking.

As we explore how this process works, you'll gain—and retain—your power when you can hide your emotional buttons. When everyone can see these poking out, you're easy to agitate, and thus to control. Remember, the goal is to be Teflon. Let it all slide off, no matter how effective an insult may be.

"That's the ugliest red shirt I've ever seen in my life!" I can't tell you how many times I've used this line to point out to people their over-reaction to things that don't matter. The line works best because the person I'm saying this to is not even wearing a red shirt. (However, it was hilarious when I tried using this with a client, not realizing he was color blind, and he said, "Is it? I'm color blind. I can't tell..." Touché, Anthony, touché!)

Often, the automatic reaction is to get upset and defend against the criticism. That is, until they realize their shirt isn't even red. Their face turns red—involuntarily, preparing for battle—before the reality lands that their shirt isn't even red. Then I reply, "Right. Like most criticisms of you, they aren't true. So why respond?" The secret is, we aren't responding to the *accuracy* of the criticism; we're responding to the *insult*. Like, we must defend ourselves from things that aren't true.

Going back to the red shirt analogy, there are two other points that should be added to the fact that the shirt isn't red. First, you like the shirt. Why isn't that good enough? Well, maybe because you were teased as a child and are sensitive to the acceptance of others. But, fuck it. You like the shirt. That seems good enough.

The other point is, "Who the hell am I?" I mean, yeah, they do come to my office for my help. I'm a professional, so my opinion matters...but does it matter more than your own opinion of yourself?

That's pretty stupid. It doesn't. Others' opinions and ideas about us are useful, but only up to a point. But what point?

The point at which someone else's ideas about us touch the third rail of our deeply held insecurities, in which someone else's external voice echoes the worst things we think and feel about ourselves. This is why we're doing all of this work to understand our anger: Chances are, our anger is a reaction to what feels bad, and only by examining all of this can we figure out how to override these feelings so we don't react with anger. It reminds me of when I was young and macho and tried to convince myself and anyone else, "I don't give a shit what anyone thinks of me!" Ah...the bravado. The feigned indifference. The cloak of invulnerability and invincibility. The pounding of the chest that insecure males engage in.

The truth is, the only way this idea is true—that we don't give a *shit*—is if you don't have any relationships that matter to you. If you care about people, you care about their opinions. Those people in your inner circle, their opinions matter. The people on whom you depend and who value you, their perspectives are important. The average kid on the street shouldn't, at least not much.

I think the easiest way to think of it is this: Yeah, people's opinions matter. People who are close to you, whom you love and who care about you, who look out for your best interests, they can impact your opinion of yourself. Your personal integrity cannot be so fragile that it collapses under the weight of criticism from irrelevant people. Get better at seeing what and who matter, and what and who you have the delicious privilege of completely ignoring.

Ninety-nine percent of conflicts can be avoided, and tons of anger can be dodged, when we just take a fraction of a second to realize that in nearly *all* cases, no response is the right one. This has nothing to do with you. You can sidestep all kinds of stupid drama and dumb, angry overreacting by raising the bar of what qualifies as "irrelevant" in your life. Hint: It's virtually everything. And even if it's not irrelevant, will you really care about it two weeks from now? If this isn't important enough to be an issue down the line, usually it's worth letting it die on the vine. Save your strength, save your breath, and keep walking. Or, as is sometimes said, "Don't accept criticism from people you would not seek advice from."

* * *

For some people, it may be very difficult to identify their indirect triggers on their own. It may require exploring them in therapy. Which is worth mentioning. In 2025, though there is some modicum of improvement, there is still tremendous stigma related to being in therapy. I often joke that it's similar to medications and natural childbirth; everyone seems to be okay using drugs except when they should be. Delivering a bowling ball through a tiny hole fucking hurts. Passing a kidney stone generates the closest appreciation of serious pain a man can relate to. During these times, pain meds make sense.

Similarly, everyone wants to talk about their issues in non-therapeutic environments, post them on Facebook or Instagram, and wait for the world's validation...or gossip about everything going on in someone's life. But, when it comes to talking about their innermost struggles, then...then they become concerned that people might think that they're crazy, or unstable, or not *totally* in control of themselves, or even worse: have normal, human vulnerabilities, insecurities, messed-up boundaries or experiences that trouble them, or create uncertainty.

Or they can't afford therapy, but they have $20,000 in credit card debt (and don't get me started on college loans). Or they overpay on a monthly car payment, yet they don't have the money to invest in their own sanity. Therapy is an investment. When done right, it should not be a ten-year process (unless you're interested in the long-term existential, psychodynamic examination of your earliest personality development and figuring out how to right the ship). The goal of therapy should always be to end therapy. It need not be a permanent relationship, any more than an orthopedist is: get in, work through some issues, gain a better understanding, heal, and use these new muscles and strengths out in the world.

So far, we've looked at your relationship with yourself. But who are we kidding? We're hardly alone in the world. The billions of other people here are also having relationships with themselves. And some of them are involved in relationships with you. This is where the rubber meets the road of controlling the flame: with the people we care about. We know now that in most cases, we can stay chilled, since we don't have to care and certainly don't have to react to what other people are saying and doing. But what about that small group of people who actually matter?

PARTNERS, PARENTS, AND KIDS

Ah...relationships. The biggest and often messiest part of our lives. We all have them, even those among us who have checked out of relating to other people and live in relative seclusion. Usually, they did this because of relationships.

How do you talk about triggers and not appreciate the fact that these three groups of people piss you off the most? Yeah, there are some among us who are chronically angry people who lash out at the turtle crossing the road (or any other innocent victim). But even the calmest people find a way to ruin their reputations by overreacting to sweet, little old Nana, who tells you to put your sweater on one too many times.

Or your three-year-old, well-dressed, cute-as-a-button son whom everyone adores, and you secretly have moments when you wish someone, anyone, could get him to shut the hell up. Or your father, who always bails you out when your car breaks down but has the audacity to tell one too many "dad jokes," like your nerves are being stretched to the breaking point of your patience. Oh...and your doting husband or attentive wife...they're always saints. Though people often get married or partner up because of the great characteristics the other person brings to the table, you could make a good argument that the lasting success of a relationship will rest on the ability to tolerate, if not appreciate, the things that might drive some people nuts.

There must be some normalization of conflict in relationships. The fact that there are arguments is not the problem; it's how they are resolved. The only way two people won't have disagreements is if they never listen to one another. No matter how great one's characteristics may be, they can get overshadowed by annoying ones. It was once said, "You show me the most beautiful woman in the world, and I'll show you a guy who can't stand her." And this is true for men and women.

What do these groups all have in common? Is it that you're really a misanthrope who covertly hates everyone around you? Well, I guess maybe...but not likely. Is it that relationships are so hard that no matter how you try, people are going to annoy you—and enrage you—from time to time? Yes! Of course...but that ain't it either. People who spend a lot of time with you know you like the back of their hands. Your parents have been watching you since you arrived. And even the most affectionate parent who soothes the booboo on your knee also figures out, perhaps unconsciously, the things that piss you off.

Let me also add that when you have problems in a single relationship, like your marriage, and nowhere else, you don't have an anger management problem. You have a relationship problem. Yes, skills to identify your pending anger and calm you down before you do something problematic is helpful, but if you only have problems in one domain of your life, the problem is in that domain. An anger management problem is a theme where you have difficulty holding your shit together in multiple places, with multiple people, across multiple times.

Your kids? Are you kidding me? They've been literally watching you since they opened their eyes for the first time. Whether you like it or not, you taught them how to be human. They know your subtleties. They recognize your idiosyncrasies. They pick up your mood changes from a change in your facial expression to the tone of your voice to a disruption in your energy. You know what else they learn? When to not fuck with Mom! Like, I'm not saying kids are saints, but even when they're mischievous, they know when they just pushed a bit too far, and there's a good chance that they will seriously piss off their parents...or as is the catch phrase these days: F-A-F-O. Fuck around and find out!

Socially intelligent people, including those in the above groups, recognize which alleys to avoid walking down. Yep, go ahead and say anything other than "Thanks, Dad" when he cooked dinner after working a double shift, while Mom is still at work, and he's doing the best he can. Go ahead, I dare you! I bet you get a look that even Clint Eastwood would be proud of.

We pay attention to the people we spend the most time with and care the most about. If people know your buttons—especially better than you do—they learned them from studying you. You don't study people you don't care about. So, if they have your number, you gave it to them and taught them how to press your buttons. The hope is that they care about you enough to not provoke you. The other part of it is that you have your buttons hidden well enough that even when people are trying to get you going, you don't blow up so quickly. The last thing you need, especially on a day that hasn't gone your way, is your buttons standing out so prominently that you look like a porcupine.

Now, this is still an oversimplification because there are many reasons why people argue with those who are close to them, but as we're talking about trigger recognition, you give them the keys to the castle when they know your buttons...so identify them and keep them better protected.

Maybe you're still wondering what I'm talking about. What are these indirect triggers he's talking about?

One trigger I have is that it pisses me off when I don't feel appreciated. I work hard to try to be a generous person. I enjoy taking care of people around me and showing them a good time. Some of it's because I grew up poor and, now doing better, it's a reminder of how far I've come when I can pay for entertainment for those I care about. I also love a good time. I love to laugh...and argue...and laugh while arguing. Add a cigar and some bourbon after a nice steak dinner, and I'm golden.

I'm also a protector, and I want those around me to know that they can relax and just chill and have a good time. They are safe. Very, very few things can't be said out loud. I hope they're happy and comfortable, because I am, and I want them to feel at ease. I can achieve that by using my physical presence or my group of friends, who can "ensure" that things don't get out of control.

The point is, when I give and care as much as I can for the people I love, I'm not looking for pomp and circumstance, but a "thank you" goes miles. When doing many things that I don't have to do in order to make people around me happy, I want them to enjoy themselves. I don't want to be taken for granted. Now the truth of the matter is, if I want them to be happy, then them being happy is the thank you. Or maybe, on this particular day, they're so caught up with their own shit that they don't even realize my efforts. It's my issue, not theirs. If I can't survive without some gratitude, then don't put so much effort in, Mitch... Well, I'm working on it.

The point is that I have come to appreciate that when I feel taken for granted, it pisses me off. Sometimes more than seems reasonable, but this bit of being taken for granted starts to feel like being taken advantage of. So, I work on that. I realize that is the dynamic I'm vulnerable to, and I try to shore it up when it unfolds, rather than allowing it to build under the surface and become more prone to exploding outward. I know it's an issue for me. Learn your issues and work on them.

There are themes that we see. Some of them are along gender lines, and our partners may weaponize them. A woman may be accused of being a gold-digger, only interested in a man for what he can give them materially, versus the quality of the relationship. They can be accused of being dumb or intellectually inferior—more bullshit. Some men continue to wish this were true, so much so that it has been attempted to be spoken into existence. Women who are independent or self-sufficient must be man-hating and will grow to be lonely shrews.

Women are labeled flaky and hypocritical because of their superficiality with their preference for brand-name items and plastic surgery; yet, they've been socialized to value appearance over all else since they were toddlers. Of note, what do rich men do more and more? Buy name-brand items, making sure the logos are clearly visible, and increasingly consider plastic surgery. Why? Because it is not about genitals. It is about the insecurity and desire to be desired, to be seen as attractive or valued. Most of us deal with that on some level.

For men, as comedian Christopher Titus pointed out after an argument with his ex-wife, when they argue, she goes for the classics: "Your dick's too small," "You're stupid," and (hitting him below the belt) "You're not funny!"

The line that runs through all of this is the issue of inadequacy—that one's sexual virility, ability to earn money, or ability to have a meaningful conversation are the only things that make someone have some value. Yet, at the end of it all, whatever pushes your buttons, you should know about them and work on them. If you don't, you're easily provokable and therefore weak. That is why indirect triggers are so important.

USE OF CUES

It is undeniable that trigger recognition assists with anger management. You know something is annoying you, you see it, and you start to de-escalate before getting too pissed and doing something destructive. What if there is a related skill that is similar and can be used as a prequel? After all, there are times we get surprised or caught off guard by things upsetting us. And, as I discussed before, if we wait for our body to respond to let us know we're getting angry, especially in sports where our nervous system is going to start accelerating in the heat of the battle anyway, it could be too late when we start to adjust the flame.

For that reason, it is helpful for us to utilize cues as a reminder to calm ourselves down when we are entering into an environment that we know may be stressful. Cues are similar to triggers in that they should get you doing something for a particular reason.

It's common, when I'm working with a basketball player shooting free throws, for me to instruct her to look at the center of the box right above the rim. I ask her to use her skills to recenter herself when she sees that. That may mean taking two or three deep breaths to ground herself, or going through some familiar routine, like how many dribbles she takes with the ball before preparing for the shot. But, the cue that reminds her to do this is that box on the backboard. Why do I use that? Because every backboard has that sweet spot marked right behind the rim, usually in white tape or paint, and she will be able to use that cue in her environment to remind her to take control of her body and adjust the flame.

Dr. Ken Ravizza was one of the pioneers of sport psychology and worked with many successful baseball teams. When working with Evan Longoria, former star third baseman for the Tampa Rays, Ken taught him something brilliant. Whenever he felt his emotions were out of control, step out of the batter's box and focus on the top of the left field foul pole. Why was this such a useful cue? Because he knew every field has a left field foul pole. That makes the cue portable. Anywhere he goes, Longoria could use this technique. And he would: step out, take a couple of breaths, reset, and attack the next play.

External cues are useful reminders. What do you do if you're an executive and there is no foul pole? Or a mother who just got home from work and isn't looking at a backboard on a basketball court? There are two options: either identify your own cue that will be where you are likely to be irritated, or create your own cues.

What could that cue be? Whatever will remind you to implement your de-escalation tools and get you back to baseline before blowing up at something disproportionately because you expect a confrontation. It could be the center of the steering wheel of your car before you go into your house. It could be the fan in your bedroom when you are changing out of your clothes before interacting with your family after a long day. It could be the upper right corner of your computer monitor before you go to the boardroom for a meeting. It can be *anything*—so long as you identify it and utilize it as *your* cue, to cool your jets and put you in the best position to read and react.

The other option for making your own cues is something that I developed with players over twenty years ago. There is always a way that you can create a portable cue to take with you. I had baseball players write a letter on each of their batting gloves to remind them of their plan. For example, they wrote "S" on their left to cue them for smooth, indicating time to relax, and then on the other glove, "E" for explode. This symbolized the calm before the storm. Reset, chill a bit, step back in, and aggressively attack the play.

I have done it for parents during divorce mediations, asking them to hold a wallet-sized picture (when people actually had those...now, I ask them to pull it up on their phones) in their hands to remind them what/who really matters here. Their kids. "So, don't get so angry and emotional that you make bad decisions for your children. Relax and focus on the matter at hand," I advised them.

The ultimate message about cues is that there are times when we know stress is coming. Some of that will trigger anger. Some may trigger fear or other feelings. We can place cues in our environment as a reminder to calm ourselves *before* the trigger arrives, so we are not primed for conflict, but already more emotionally balanced and able to utilize our minds to solve problems without the negative impact rage may have.

9

COGNITIVE RESTRUCTURING: LOSING YOUR SHIT MAKES YOU DUMB AND POTENTIALLY DANGEROUS

Have you ever noticed how fucking stupid you become when you're in a rage? We talked about this earlier, but I mean really "off-the-chart moron" stupid. Everyone has had this experience, where they're in an argument and they think they're winning, so they get more and more pissed and immediately start losing the argument.

There's that old Yerkes-Dodson Law again—as anger goes up, there's a point where performance goes down...and that's because your body shifts to survival mode, not to doing calculus. And if you happen to be married to a woman who has the memory of an elephant and can recall events accurately in a manner that only a computer can, you, my friend, are screwed...at least if you think you're going to win the argument. In fact, you probably won't be literally screwed any time soon either because in your desperation, you say shit that should never be said...and that cannot be easily taken back.

If we're going to highlight how poorly your brain works when you're really angry, we need to discuss problem-solving issues, because they represent the before and after, the initiator and consequence of rage. That is to say that people become frustrated when they can't solve problems, and that pisses them off. And when they get infuriated, they become even worse at solving problems. Thus, shoring up these skills puts one at an advantage to be more effective, before, during, and after getting incensed.

Something else to consider, coming from someone who hasn't won an argument with my wife...like ever: I personally don't like apologizing. It's no fun for me. It can be embarrassing to have to own the wrongness of your position out loud. Now, don't get me wrong. It is important to do so, but I don't like it. So...I work *really hard* to avoid doing things I'll have to apologize for. While checkers is played move to move, chess is played by anticipating strategies several moves down the line. Learn to play chess!

This does not even consider the fact that basic problem-solving skills are surprisingly absent from a lot of people's toolboxes. And, they are relatively easy to teach. Problem-solving rests on a fairly simple process (although it's a lot harder to describe it).

Break down the details of a scenario you're facing. The more practice you have in making these quick assessments, the easier it will be.

* * *

The Five Ws and H:
- Who?
- What?
- When?
- Where?
- Why?
- How?

These fundamental factors teach us a lot about a situation, highlight the circumstances when we struggle, and can show us opportunities to improve things. They're the questions asked in the Hassle Logs we talked about earlier in the book, and by breaking things down, we can generate solutions on how to handle things better. My experience has taught me that the *Why* and *How* are more important than all of the other factors.

Sure, *who* is interesting. Are there certain people you find yourself irritable around often? If so, figure out the *why*. Are there times of the day (maybe when you're hungry or your brain has not fully booted up yet) when you're cranky? And then there's *where*. Are you someone who goes nuts in noisy, chaotic restaurants, or do you thrive in that hive of activity or energy? Do you dread certain events? If so, buckle up, because there are all kinds of things in life we can't avoid, but we can prepare so we don't have the kinds of relationship-melting reactions many of us are prone to.

Let's focus on *why*. Why did that person do what they did? Why did it piss you off (or more aptly, why did you become angry in response to it)? Why now? This has happened a hundred other times, but today you lost your shit over it. *Why?*

How...how did they do things in a way that provoked you, when someone else did the same thing and you didn't flinch? Often, we find errors in thinking. We read nonverbal cues as personal dismissals. A roll of the eyes. A suck of the teeth. A back turned away. Focusing on a phone while you're in the middle of a discussion. How did this person's actions precede your irritation?

It is not just the breakdown of the components of the problem that are useful, but also discerning how getting angry did not help you solve the problem. This is our tendency to have a certain distorted "cognitive set" that contributes to the issues. That is the hostility bias we spoke about earlier. And, the aspects of the hostility bias can be changed by restructuring the way we think about the world and situations, leading to a better understanding. When we have a clearer picture of our cognitive set, we know what we're dealing with—in other people and in ourselves.

* * *

Humans have lots of thoughts that just don't make sense. We call these "cognitive distortions," and sometimes they're learned. Often, they're rooted in our deepest, earliest unresolved issues with our parents, and overall, if we don't try to challenge our thinking and offer alternatives, we're going to be stuck in patterns of irritation.

Perhaps the most common distortion is the "just world" fallacy. Though most mothers admonished their child with "Well, life isn't fair!" in response to the child's frustration with a perceived inequality that challenged their sense of right and wrong, the message doesn't sink in. Isn't it presumptuous for us to think that things are supposed to be a certain way? And when things don't go the way we want, we have a temper tantrum about it. We regress from mature adults to two-year-olds stomping our feet because things didn't go the way we wanted. Who fucking said that the world has to be convenient to you and things must go the way you want? No one. But, how you respond to these situations determines who is in charge. We may have very little control over nearly everything around us, but we control ourselves, or are trying to.

Albert Ellis, who developed Rational Emotive Behavior Therapy, often talked about how we put demands on ourselves that are not rooted in reality. In a very high-pitched, nasally voice, in response to someone talking about what they believed they had to do, he would say, "It would be nice...you may prefer it. *But, it's not gonna kill ya if it doesn't happen.*" He described this as the "Tyranny of the Shoulds," how we get dominated by demands that are not life and death issues. Being particularly pedantic and crafty with words, he coined some funny phrases to challenge one's irrational thoughts. Some of these include, "Don't SHOULD on yourself" and "Don't engage in MUSTurbatory behavior." These thought criticisms don't easily leave your mind after you hear them for the first time.

"GOOD!" said Jocko Willink. Willink is a retired U.S. Navy SEAL officer, leadership consultant, author, and podcast host. He served as the commander of SEAL Team 3, Task Unit Bruiser, one of the most decorated units in the Iraq War. He's known for his hardcore discipline, leadership philosophy, and motivation, often emphasizing personal responsibility and mental toughness. He's a certifiable badass!

In a particularly powerful video clip, he talked about "Good." No matter the situation that faced him, his response was often "Good!" Because, as he wisely pointed out, no matter the situation, there's always some good that comes from it if you look for it. You get hurt?

Good. You will learn resilience and build other parts of your body. You didn't get the promotion? Good. It may not have been the best fit for you anyway. You get fired? Good. Now you can focus on going where your passion was going to take you, but you did not pursue it because you were focused on something else.

As long as you can say "Good!" you're still alive and still have some fight in you. So get your shit together and refocus yourself. Reorient your view of what is possible. Accept when something didn't happen, when you didn't get what you wanted, or when something feels unjust. Reposition your strength and energy to think differently about what's happening in that moment.

The first time I saw that video clip, I was ready to run through a wall. He triggered a very basic concept for me. Most of what we want is out there to get *if* we go get it. If we refuse to be denied or beaten down by outside factors, or if we allow antiquated ideas, like the world has to be fair, to dictate what we can do in life, we remain stuck and facing backward. I want the people I work with to examine the past for areas of improvement, but not to get trapped there. After getting a handle on the past, forward is the only direction. It's where the good, the new, and the untried and untested lie, and when you're not fucking angry, getting there is much easier, smoother, and more fun.

PREDICTION OF CONSEQUENCES

Every time I start talking about the prediction of consequences, people look at me like I'm crazy. I'm not saying I'm not crazy; we all are. However, people largely don't appreciate how predictable life often is, and we can use this as a method to avoid conflicts in life.

When I was growing up in the 1990s, singer Dionne Warwick, and later Ms. Cleo, hosted infomercials for the Psychic Friends Network (PFN). The infomercials featured "psychic" Linda Georgian and offered viewers the opportunity to call a psychic for a reading. This was way before caller ID and cellphones. I often joked to myself that if I called them and they didn't say, "Hey Mitch, I knew you were going to call," I'd hang up, unimpressed with their true psychic ability to tell fortunes and predict the future.

Then, over the course of time, I became curious about how different people, including James Randi, who died in 2020, were able to debunk many paranormal claims of psychics, fortune tellers, mediums, etc., as frauds. He offered a million dollars to any of them who could prove their powers existed under controlled circumstances. No one ever won the money. Yet, it had no impact on people paying a lot of money to have these readings.

My point here is not to argue about whether paranormal abilities exist. Rather, it's the opposite. If people can predict the future, they can avoid problems in their lives. I do not believe all people can predict all things. However, I am damn sure that we can predict more things than we realize. Either because we have an understanding of statistics and probabilities or because we understand rules that set the expectations of certain circumstances.

For example, consider a coin. You flip it and you have a 50/50 chance of getting a head. Even if you have ten heads in a row, you still have a 50/50 chance on the eleventh, but as we continue our efforts and understand the rule of large numbers, we will regress to the mean. In fact, the longer you go with heads, the more likely future flips will yield a tail.

If someone is truly a 35 percent three-point shooter in basketball, without even considering standard deviation, which would tell us a bit about their "scatter" (how streaky they are), if she hits ten in a row, she will eventually start missing and regress toward her average of 35 percent.

Using this logic, if you go up to a cop and punch them in the face, what do you believe will happen? Most people respond, "I'll get arrested..." If you're lucky, all that will happen is that you get arrested. How do we know that? Because it's predictable.

If you get angry and yell at your kid after they come and tell you that they just colored on the wall, what will they do in the future? Maybe they won't color on the wall. It is also possible they won't tell you next time, which is the more likely outcome.

Or maybe at work you find yourself easily irritated at your subordinates. Perhaps you mock them for doing their tasks poorly. They then don't want to work so hard for you, and your team's productivity goes down. Then it's the end of the year and your supervisor is going to meet with you about bonuses. Your numbers are down, your team's morale is visibly deflated, and they've complained about you to HR and your boss. Please predict for me the likelihood of you getting a big bonus. Slim, *at best*.

Clearly, the point is that while we can't predict the future about everything, there are many things that we can see coming around the corner. And usually, when we're spilling our anger out on everyone around us, it doesn't increase positive opportunities for us. We're much better served by considering the possible responses we have to a given situation, weighing how our anger impacts both our decision-making and the implementation of our choice for the best course of action, and making the decisions that can give us the best chance of success.

Prediction of consequences is a skill that can be learned *and* improved upon. It's important in relationships. It's important in school. It's important in sports. It's important on the job. If you want to learn how to control your anger, you need to improve your ability to predict the future, then use that information in the context of modulating your emotions to get the results you are looking for in life.

10

RAGE ROOMS & OTHER DEAD ENDS

I can't count how many times I've heard self-anointed anger management experts give the horrible advice of "Well, if you get angry, just punch a heavy punching bag" or "Yell into a pillow and you will feel so much better." The reason this is horrible advice is because they are right. You will feel better.

Catharsis, which is the fancy word for releasing pent-up psychological tension, works. Instinctively, we understand this. At the end of the day, with all your pressures that have built up, you feel like you have a spring compressed inside of you, or you feel like a pressure cooker ready to explode. This happens because we don't de-escalate after every time something pisses us off during the day. This again is the explosion threshold I spoke of earlier in the book.

There's a cumulative effect that our body keeps track of. We long to have that released. And there are many ways to do that. The issue is that when you do punch something or scream into the pillow, you'll feel better, and that feeling better will reinforce whatever behavior you used to relieve the tension. So, if you hit the heavy punching bag and give yourself a good workout, even if you feel better afterward, you're also going to have reinforced punching as a way to solve your problems. What happens next time when you don't have a punching bag but have your partner or adversary in front of you? You will be more prone to punch.

Don't hear this as a mixed message. It is good to release this tension. But I teach people to *sublimate,* which is catharting in a socially acceptable way—and not in a way that will lead to further problems for you. Few things are more cathartic than exercise and physical activity. I absolutely encourage people to exercise regularly and rigorously, to decrease the pent-up tension they carry. Regular exercise decreases baseline levels of depression, anxiety, and anger. I do not, however, recommend any striking exercises as a way to take the edge off when someone is tense, and particularly when they know that they're angry, because then they will revert to striking in a moment when they have less control.

The same principle applies to yelling. You're pissed off and you've learned that yelling makes you feel better, right? Great…but what will that translate into when you're angry and your boyfriend is in front of you? A propensity to yell. You may feel better by releasing the energy, but you will also be less likely to communicate effectively, and that may hurt the feelings of someone you care about in your moment of "catharsis."

For people who are struggling with anger, the following exercise modalities are useful: aerobics, spinning, Zumba, yoga, swimming, weight training (both explosive and lower weight/high reps), running (both sprinting and longer distances), elliptical machines, CrossFit, biking, jumping rope, calisthenics, and nearly every other exercise. Clearly, what's not on this list is one-on-one fighting. What I would recommend avoiding is sparring, hitting the heavy bag, other striking exercises, and MMA work. Not so coincidentally, there is some evidence of higher incidence of domestic violence in the MMA community, while other athlete populations have *not* been proven to be more violent than their non-athlete peers.

This isn't just anecdotal; it's our biology: When someone learns this one way to react, they're obviously disinclined to sit down with a soothing cup of tea to really talk about how they're feeling. Having honed the most violent and aggressive part of themselves in years of practice, they use this tool in nearly every circumstance.

We see catharsis spoofed in *Analyze This* when Billy Crystal's psychiatrist character, Dr. Ben Sobel, encourages Robert De Niro's mafioso, Paul Vitti, to let off some steam by hitting a pillow, leading De Niro to respond by pulling out a gun and firing several rounds into the couch. Dr. Sobel asks, "Feel better?" Vitti replies, "Yeah...I do," as feathers fly everywhere from the "whacked" pillow.

* * *

As I'm sure you have as well, I've seen ads for Rage Rooms that "guarantee to cure you of your anger problems!" First, let me say, we Americans will buy literally anything, so I'm not surprised that there's a marketplace for our anger. Rage Rooms that purport to cure your anger problems by giving you a place to "safely" express your anger by breaking things with bats, sledgehammers, and other weapons of destruction, make for good theater. By the way, they say you can do this safely while you also have to sign releases that exonerate the owners of the premises if you die while you are "curing" your anger. Interestingly, Rage Rooms might even have some value for people who believe that expressing anger at any time is bad and are thus constantly suppressed. Many owners note that, to their surprise, most of their clientele are women and executives in positions that seem too sophisticated to want to engage in primal catharsis.

That being said, the idea that Rage Rooms cure anger problems is unabashedly bullshit. They do not do anything to cure anger. As mentioned above, there's no reason to believe that people who exert their anger outward are going to "run out" of anger and leave it all there, in broken plates and shattered glass. In fact, chronically angry people are usually easily provoked, physiologically high-strung, and find even neutral stimuli as a justification to fight, so guess what? They do. In fact, Rage Rooms create the opportunity for the reinforcement of breaking things. Destruction of things can easily generalize to destruction of people's property, and then in turn destruction of people. Rage Rooms should be seen simply as an entertainment complex with no therapeutic value because that's all they are: noisy, theatrical destruction for people who like breaking shit.

To expand on this issue to nearly comical proportions, I'm sure you've noticed the opportunity to throw axes in bars and restaurants near you. Notwithstanding the nostalgic consideration of lumberjacks waxing poetic about the beauty of a well-balanced ax that hits its mark reliably, this is similar to going to the shooting range to fire guns, with a couple of exceptions.

One: Shooting ranges have close oversight by trained instructors who will quickly expel anyone who is not staying clearly inside the rules. Two: Firearms are more lethal than axes. Axes are not easily wielded and are somewhat awkward, and people don't generally carry axes for self-defense, nor are they employed by law enforcement. Perhaps most importantly, however, you will never hear that alcohol is served at a firing range, where getting tanked is followed by handling deadly firearms. For fun. Ax-throwing sites not only allow alcohol but encourage its consumption. How long did it take before a site had its liquor license suspended due to a drunk patron throwing an ax at someone else? Not long. And why is anyone surprised? These things have no business being present in the same place.

Why is this so problematic? Alcohol, besides severely impacting your physical coordination, significantly impairs your impulse control. My years spent bouncing in bars and clubs proved beyond a shadow of a doubt that drunk people are much stupider than sober people, and often are more dangerous. The part of your brain responsible for stopping you from doing dumb things is the first to go offline under the influence of alcohol. So...throwing axes and drinking alcohol...what could go wrong? Imagine if alcohol were available in a Rage Room. It's a natural extension of ax-throwing to progress to Rage Rooms.

While we're talking about alcohol, let's consider its role in violence in the home. What percent of domestic violence cases are believed to have alcohol as a contributing factor? Studies vary, but the World Health Organization estimates that roughly 55 percent of domestic abuse perpetrators were drinking prior to assault. Clearly, drinking and anger that leads to violence go hand in hand. Surely, you've heard of someone being described as an "angry drunk." Is there anyone less pleasant to invite over? The predictability of their now unrepressed rage, which has transformed this ordinarily affable and fun friend into an uncontrollable beast on a hair-trigger, conscripts everyone around them to slow them down. We can feel when they're about to go over the edge and the trouble will start. Since alcohol amplifies emotion, while also disinhibiting the person, the angry drunk needs to stop drinking.

11

PARENTING
WHEN ANGRY

Those who engage in spanking and corporal punishment have struggled with this issue. There is no doubt at this point that corporal punishment, especially when it is extreme and utilized while the parent is angry, has the potential for abuse. This is because under those circumstances, the angry parent is engaging in reactive aggression and wants to hurt the child, which can be a recipe for disaster.

Corporal punishment has been universally tarnished as an unacceptable form of discipline. My humble opinion is that corporal punishment is *not* the equivalent of abuse. At times when corporal punishment was utilized more universally in the United States, children developed greater respect (if not fear) of their parents, teachers, and other authority figures. There is little evidence to support that today's youth are more docile and respectful and/or less rebellious and dangerous than children of previous generations. Why? Because too many parents utilized corporal punishment at times. They were angry and legitimately abused their children, while we collectively ignored and disregarded the parents who appropriately used corporal punishment (as well as other methods) to shape their children's behavior.

Thus, was corporal punishment the problem or was it "merely" the vehicle of what happens when parents try to discipline when they are angry? I would argue the latter.

Remove corporal punishment and replace it with solely verbal intervention and you will find some parents yelling, screaming obscenities, and abusing their children in other ways. Punishment and discipline are to teach children accountability and how to act, to decrease certain behaviors and to prevent the recurrence of unacceptable behavior. It is not meant to be punitive and hurtful. Anger, when not modulated, can spill discipline from punishment to being punitive. This is another place where anger rears its head and society can't separate the forest from the trees.

A couple of other points about parenting when angry: There is probably no better way to completely sabotage effective discipline than to do it when you're furious. Why? Well, the simplest answer is that your brain turns off when you're that pissed. You'll see parents yelling at their kids. Making practically no sense. Contradicting themselves from sentence to sentence. Leaving the children completely confused about what their folks are saying. And the worst is when, while angry, they threaten the most ridiculous things. DO NOT BLUFF WHEN YOU ARE PARENTING. So when you say, "That's it! You're grounded for six months!!!," as a parent, you just shit the bed.

Why? Well, first off, what would a child have to do wrong that merits a six-month punishment? Second, let's say you did forbid your child from doing anything they want—no socialization, not going anywhere, just staying in the house for six months. Who exactly are you punishing? Them...or you? So, they'll go to their rooms and scroll on their phones or play video games (unless you take them too), probably mope around fairly miserably. Now they're home as a constant reminder of your over-the-top punishment and potentially in the way of you doing what you want to.

Further, the punishment needs to fit the crime. It should be proportional to the wrongness or the seriousness of the child's misdeed. There should be a temporal relationship between the offending behavior and the punishment. It should be quick, fair, and appropriate for the problem behavior. Excessively long punishment misses the boat. It needs to sting but not leave a mark—except for the lesson being learned. If your daughter is scrolling on her phone and not getting up to empty the dishwasher when you ask her to, taking her phone for a night or two makes the point.

Your son beats up his little brother—not in the normal horseplay that anxious mothers believe always leads to ER trips, but a disproportionate situation, where the little brother is hurt (and did not have it coming to him by hitting the older kid with a stick first). Guess what: You're not playing in tonight's basketball game. "But my team needs me!" your son may plead. And it is perfectly fine to say, "The expectations of how we will treat one another in this house exceed your extracurriculars. I've made this clear. Now I'm enforcing it."

If kids don't receive consequences for their behavior, do not be surprised when they think they don't have any rules that they have to follow.

As I've often said to my kids, "If I yell, you should listen. If I whisper, you should worry." Kids know, especially if their parents are not inclined to hit them, that parents yelling is often empty noise. In fact, many mothers get frustrated when their children don't respond to their yelling. If you scream all the time, the kids lose the ability to tell when Mom is just losing her shit again or if this is a legitimate issue and I need to take it down...because she means business.

But when I'm whispering, I'm calm. I'm in control. And I will figure out what punishment will get the results I am looking for. As you have seen as a theme throughout this book, you want to harness your anger, and frankly, when you're that pissed off, you won't make good decisions as a disciplinarian. So, recognize that you're getting hot, take a couple of minutes to de-escalate yourself, consult with your partner about potential options, and calmly let the kids know you mean business and that they don't want to test you...then mete out the appropriate discipline.

I refer back to *Monsters, Inc.* and Sully, our large, furry monster who is particularly good at scaring kids. No one wants to be Sully. No one wants their children to be terrified of them, whimpering, and hiding in a corner for protection. Effective parenting requires that children know their parents are serious and will set limits, but the limits will not be so harsh that they'll be scared or scarred. Effective parenting utilizes padded fences. They are sturdy and will provide boundaries that don't bend, but when you run into them, you don't get destroyed either.

When disciplining children, it's very important that parents be intentional and consistent about it. This is not easy to do. There are so many distractions, and children change every day, so it sometimes feels like we're dealing with a brand new child every morning. The goal of discipline is to teach and to change behavior, not to hurt the child, of course. One tool that is often used is one's voice. I remember once when my son Logan was about four years old. He thought it was a good idea to mouth off to his mother. To this day, I don't know what it was about and my wife and son barely remember the situation; but, I do... I just knew the tone was all wrong. The volume was too loud for him to be yelling at his mother that way.

I went upstairs to tend to something else when I heard the commotion. Even though I'm a big guy, I can move pretty quietly for my size, and he was so busy being a brat that he didn't hear me come down the stairs. I was standing behind him as he was squawking at my wife, and I have to admit, I was surprised that this kid had the balls to do this. But I knew what he didn't: He underestimated what his mother was capable of. Shit, *I* don't have the courage to talk to her that way. He needed an intervention, and quickly, before things got out of hand.

I knew that I was going to raise my voice, yell at him, probably scare the shit out of him, and then send him to his room to think about what he was doing. The problem was that my daughter, Aviva, who was about six years old at the time, was looking at me as I was preparing to "have a short chat" with my son. Remembering the scene with Sully, I did not want her terrified of me, like Boo had been. I could see that she was not sure what was about to happen, but the tension was visible in her body language. I realized that while I wanted to get Logan's attention with my tone of voice, I was in complete control, but I didn't want her to be scared. Knowing that my voice was going to be loud and deep enough to shake the walls, I winked at Aviva so she knew that everything was going to be okay. That wink changed everything. She uncoiled, relaxing slightly, knowing it would be loud but not terrifying.

I was getting ready to "speak" with my son, my wife was looking at him in disbelief, and my daughter began to smile, because she realized this had the potential to be freaking hilarious.

"Logan!" I yelled from behind him. It was like his soul had temporarily exited his body. He was caught. He turned and looked at me with very wide eyes that communicated surprise and guilt. I got his attention, which was, of course, my plan. "You never talk to your mother that way. Now, you need to go up to your room and don't reappear until we're ready to talk to you." He walked up the stairs with his tail between his legs. Shortly thereafter, I went to his room and spoke to him calmly. In the lesson of the expectations that we had of him, I pointed out that I was not out of control. I was not in a rage. I was deliberately letting him know who was in control and that he wasn't.

The point of this story is that I was using my voice to teach a lesson. I was not trying to hurt him; I was trying to startle him and alert him that he was not in charge. He got the lesson, and though I admire his four-year-old courage and ability to assert himself, he was testing the limits of his power in the wrong way, on the wrong people, and in the wrong tone.

He was not the one with power, and the people who had power—his parents—took charge of the situation, as was necessary in that moment. It would not have had the same effect if I had hit him, which was never going to happen. My voice was more than enough for the situation. Was I angry that he was being disrespectful to his mother? Yes, absolutely. Was I so angry that I could not think straight? Absolutely not.

Parents need to be able to monitor how they're feeling and use their voices, their influence, and their creativity in dissuading children from engaging in behavior that is not good for anyone, while simultaneously not traumatizing their children so that they don't even understand or get the lesson. Fear blocks our ability to learn much of anything. Children in particular are extremely sensitive to the tone of our voices.

If you want to raise children who understand accountability, don't lose your shit when punishing them. Or, if/when you do, own it and *apologize*. Do it sincerely and try to help them understand that you know you hurt and scared them and you will not do it again. If you don't, you're teaching them that you can get angry and hurt whomever you want, without consequences. That's just bullshit. You wanted to teach them a lesson and your anger got the best of you. You didn't control the flame; you allowed it to get out of control, and you deeply regret it. "I'm sorry, son, I definitely need you to understand my expectations of you and that you will follow our rules. But I was over the top there and that defeated my purpose. So listen to the lesson, even if I need to do better at communicating with you sometimes."

Being a parent means feeling nearly constantly imperfect and ill-equipped for the role, so being able to apologize, sincerely and honestly, teaches the accountability we all hope our children learn. Kids don't come with instructional manuals. And, most parents think the instruction manual they got was for the wrong model. Sometimes parents get angry, which is understandable because we get frustrated when our kids don't act how we need or want them to. We want them to understand the consequences of their behavior, but we don't want to use anger in a way that makes them afraid of us. Besides the fact that fear makes kids less equipped to live in the world, we don't want them to be so afraid of us that they won't come to us when they need help.

* * *

But what if your kid is the one who has issues controlling their anger? Before you blame them for the programming you installed, ask yourself a few questions. Have your genetics contributed to your child's angry disposition? Yeah, probably. But as Dr. Russell Barkley has wisely noted, your child's 400+ psychological characteristics are influenced by a mosaic of their parents' genetic histories. So, it is not just from Mom or Dad, but influenced by many genetic expressions over a long period of time. And that's before the environment gets involved and installs its own set of triggers.

Neither environment nor genetics alone determines how a child's behavior will manifest itself. Parents, like shepherds (as Barkley analogized), determine the pastures that the sheep will graze, but they don't seed the soil entirely on their own. You have a great deal of influence on their nutrition, their safety, their opportunities to learn, and the challenges that will help them grow, but there will always be variables you have no control over.

Use this power wisely and improve your implementation if you have struggled with this. But it all starts with your ability to adjust your *own* flame. If you're angry, chances are that they will be too. If you're chaotic and chronically stressed out, they are likely to be as well. But if you're calm, more often than not, or at least in control of yourself, you're demonstrating what that looks like. Modeling has a tremendously powerful impact. If you're losing your shit all the time, don't be surprised when your kid does. If you are a potty mouth, don't be surprised when you hear "motherfucker" from the car seat behind you. Yeah, it's funny for a social media clip, but not so funny when a teacher, a priest, or a grandparent is disappointed in your child's behavior.

Yet, you must also be kind to yourself. You won't get it right all the time. And even if you think you've done everything right as a parent, your child still has an irritable disposition and/or acts in ways you don't like. The younger the child is, the easier it will be to implement change. Older children can have their behavior shaped, but it will take more time.

The most important thing, besides managing your own anger (there are few things harder than knowing your kid is grumpy and knowing that your grumpiness has contributed to it), is to try to understand where their anger is coming from. Everything starts with validation and correction. Just like you, your child will get angry for legitimate, frustrating reasons, and they'll overreact to relative non-issues. Validate the emotion and explore the origin. Boiling over because they lost a video game that has no real determination in their life's work is a waste of energy.

Seething because a teacher is giving tests on material that they never taught (leaving the students to feel helpless and judged, not to mention how their GPA could get screwed), or a friend betrayed them for the favor of a good-looking classmate, are understandable contributors to their anger. Remind them that not only is it okay to be angry, if you were in their situation, you would feel the same way. That last piece is really important because the ultimate validation is relatable. "I'd be just as pissed; I understand how you feel" goes a very long way.

The focus then switches to, "Okay, you have a good reason to be angry." How long do you want to stay angry, versus doing something about it? And, is this person or situation worth stealing time from your day and energy from your life? Maybe...but how much? Once you're done with holding onto your anger and frustration (and the quicker someone demands you be done, that will piss you off too and keep it going longer), you can get back to being effective.

The easiest circumstances in which to help a child are when they "simply" are lacking in anger management skills. I say "simply" because we all have to learn some new coping mechanisms. And hopefully, now that you have, you can equip your kids with tools before they need them, so you can remind them of what tool to grab when they're losing it.

If they're old enough to have reasonably developed language skills, encourage them to help you understand what is going on. Yes, it could be that anger is secondary to another feeling. A great question to ask is, "I understand you're upset about this. I don't understand why you are *this* upset about it. Can you help me get it?" They'll probably think you're asking this so you can help them, and you are, but the real value of the question is to prime them to engage their brains past just streaming emotion to getting their cognitive processes—their ability to *think*—involved. This teaches self-examination, an ability to consider the contributing factors to our feelings. Sometimes, as you see the wheels turn, they will come to the conclusion themselves that they are overreacting. Above all, this set of skills teaches children to identify their own feelings, which, as you recall, is where we started, and what so many of us are bad at doing.

Related to the above, a parent is well within their rights to tell a child, "You can be angry, but I am not tolerating you throwing things, or screaming at me, or (slot in the behavior). When you get better control of yourself, I'd be happy to sit down and talk with you."

Ahhh, but what about the child who has that hostility bias you spoke of, Dr. Abrams? Some kids wake up on the wrong side of the bed every single day, and you can't tell why. The first step is to consider that it's not a genetic disposition but instead something really bad that happened that you thought they were protected from.

Or, perhaps they have a neurophysiological condition that contributes to their presentation. ADHD remains the most over-and under-diagnosed disorder in children, as "ADHD behaviors" are multiply determined. ADHD often coexists with Oppositional Defiant Disorder and Conduct Disorder, so understanding the problems is the best chance to improve them. If there is the possibility that this could be part of the issue, get them formally assessed. I'm not a fan of throwing meds at children, and because children have great plasticity, medicating five-year-olds seems ill-advised (except for the most severe cases after a solid diagnosis). In my opinion, a proper assessment by a trained licensed psychologist is the way to go.

While we're on the topic of disorders that sometimes lead to angry, violent kids, we must consider the possibility that sometimes, something more nefarious has happened to them than we would like to admit. I talk often about the vulnerability of parenting, and that we cannot always protect our children from the world. Unfortunately, this must always be considered in the context of trauma. Hurt people hurt people, as we often hear, and it's the truth. It's how we're wired. Sometimes a child acting out is trying to tell you something, like: someone hurt me and I don't want to be a victim, so I'm going to go on the attack. We call that identification with the aggressor, and it's a common dynamic in traumatized people. Keep an eye out for this, and remain on alert for changes in a child's behavior. It's there to tell you something about their interior world.

It also may be a distraction technique. When a family is in turmoil or the environment is too chaotic, sometimes a child will act out as either a distraction or because they become the repository of the family's anger. I've seen many children, while their parents are going through hostile, scorching-the-earth, adversarial divorces, hit the gas on their anger and temper tantrums. Sometimes it will manifest itself as a "fuck it" approach to their schoolwork and their grades plummet.

Consciously or unconsciously, they're forcing the parents to shift the attention to something that the child can control. If they can get their parents to stop fighting and work together for the sake of the child, then it is a win for everyone...even though the damage the child may do to themselves in the process can sometimes be difficult to recover from.

Equally important is to focus on the behavior, not the character of the child. It is completely different to say "That behavior is a problem and it needs to stop" versus "You are a problem."

The more a parent can remain calm, not take things so personally, and approach their kid with an approach of "Okay, so you're angry. How's that working for you and what is it that you want?" without insisting on instant compliance, the better.

The problem is *not* getting angry. The problem is if it leads to destructiveness in the child and everyone around them. They can be taught the value of anger, and that getting angry is okay. It's *how* they get angry that is the issue. And *how much* anger is going to help their situation. If they're too angry to even talk about things, giving them space is fine. If you match their anger with your anger, you will do two things: teach them you're a hypocrite and that your angry behavior is allowed and theirs isn't acceptable. *And*, you will teach them to suppress their anger, for fear of consequences, instead of befriending their emotions and learning how to harness them.

If a dumb kid from Brooklyn like me can learn to make the most of their anger and use it to do great things, your kid can too. Be kind to yourself first (because you set the tone) and be kind to them, while also setting clear limits of what behavior will be allowed and what won't.

This is a very difficult topic, though, because every child is different and comes with a unique quilt of internal and externalizing qualities that are interacting. You cannot tolerate dangerous behavior. You also cannot overreact every time your child gets angry. It is, like most things in life, about balance.

12

RELATIONSHIP ISSUES: ARGUING, FIGHTING, RULES OF ENGAGEMENT, AND DOMESTIC VIOLENCE

I think of relationship issues as the fertile ground from which anger sprouts nearly universally. I don't know anyone who has been in a relationship and has never been annoyed by their partner. In fact, the only sure way to not get angry is if people don't listen to one another. If they hear where the other is coming from, inevitably there will be conflict. How do people prevent their anger from sabotaging their relationship?

The first thing you should ask yourself is whether your anger gets the best of you in most of your relationships (romantic, family, friends, work, etc.) or *just* with your spouse or partner. If it's the former, this is usually a sign of a greater problem with anger and all of the things discussed in this book, which you should try to consider, apply, and implement. It means that anger is a nearly constant presence in your life, which requires your attention as soon as possible.

If it's something that primarily comes up in your romantic relationships and nowhere else, think about why that is. Your anger does not present with your friends, family, co-workers, boss, no one else, but your partner. If that's the issue, it is not an anger issue, it is a relationship issue.

For one thing, and it's a backhanded compliment, it can mean that your partner is able to get under your skin like no one else, because they know your buttons. They've been watching you for a while and know exactly what to say or do to get you going...and not always in a good way.

The media tries to portray domestic violence as the prototypical man in a "wife-beater" t-shirt (white tank top undershirt) who comes home from work and spontaneously berates or strikes his wife. Just consider that male-on-female violence is so woven into our social consciousness that we've named an undergarment after it. Now, I'm not saying this doesn't happen (and when it does, it's horrible, inexplicable, and requires punishment and treatment), but far more common is a scene that is very different. This scene is the exception rather than the rule.

Usually, domestic violence is low-level and bidirectional—meaning that both partners are acting in abusive ways toward the other, and the behavior is comparably low-severity—screaming, cursing, maybe some physical contact (slapping or pushing), but not the extreme that requires medical and law enforcement attention. Both men and women may engage in this behavior, especially when both are heated.

Having treated thousands of perpetrators of domestic violence, most of whom have been men, the most common thing they say is, "I just wish she would have hit me. It would've hurt less than the things she said."

Very often, arguments turn violent when one of the partners feels so wronged, so insulted, or so slighted that they have to take it to a physical level in order to "right their wrong." I find that, on average, women are more socially intelligent than men and more verbally adept. Often, they're better arguers and are able to verbally eviscerate someone, and they also may figuratively hit "below the belt."

Here are the big three I've heard from patients over and over through the years: "You're no good in bed," "You can't make a living," and "You're useless" (similar to Christopher Titus' comments before). With perhaps a roll of the eyes or something equally dismissive, they communicate, "You're not a man." And for the insecure man—and, yes, most men are insecure—there may be the feeling that he has to defend his honor...even if what he's been accused of is not true.

For my male readers out there: I know how hard it is to balance healthy masculinity, power, strength, and dominance and fight back insecurity. The feelings of doubt about whether one meets our complex social expectations of what it means to be a "man" can lead to endless feelings of inadequacy. Masculinity *is* insecure, because it's so socially constructed. The stereotypes and pressures are everywhere, and they cast a long shadow over a man's self-esteem and can obviously lead to all kinds of behaviors that reflect a profound sense of insecurity. I get it. Anything can zap our confidence, fuck with our circuits, and make us react like animals—or cower and shrink. Neither feels good, and both make our lives harder.

The point I'm making is that anger in relationships is not a market that is cornered by men. Both men and women, often for reasonable reasons, get pissed at one another. The questions are: "What are the rules of engagement?" and "Can I resist the temptation to respond...

especially since this is likely to make things worse for me?"

And don't think for a second that the nonverbals don't light a fire that rages into a smoldering argument. When a woman is saying "Fine. Whatever…" while rolling her eyes or turning away…trust me… things are not fine…and she is not agreeing to your position. They are invalidations, and they can be infuriating. The same way as it is infuriating for women when a man tells her "how things are going to be," as if her opinion doesn't matter. Or when a man is hypocritical about going out with friends. He feels it's fine to go out with his friends but then gives his girlfriend a hard time, often fueled by paranoia, when she wants to see her friends, thinking she must be on the hunt for his replacement. (Yep, more insecurity).

Relationships are hard. People don't always see eye to eye, even if they love one another and see the world the same way for the most part. Now, I personally have not won a fight with my wife, ever. There are times when each of us has hit below the belt or deliberately said something to hurt the other. It's important, after the fact, to acknowledge that transgression and apologize for it. But as this certain wise woman has often said to me, "We've been together a long time. We have a family. We love each other. This shit is not going to matter in six months. We don't need to continue to fight about this."

That doesn't mean that I'm always ready to walk away from it. The truth is that it *does* feel very dismissive when she tells me an argument is over when I still have more to say. But, when we're both escalated and both pissed and increasingly not making sense, I choose to de-escalate myself. If it's really an important point or issue or area of conflict, you can always revisit it at another time when cooler heads can prevail.

You must consider whether what you're fighting about will even fucking matter down the line. To throw daggers at one another, saying things you can't take back, over issues that you won't even give a shit about weeks later, is just stupid. Give that bad habit up and let more things roll off your back. You will quickly find that less conflict about dumb shit equals more peace and happiness. After all, would you rather always be right, or be happier more of the time? I think you know the answer.

And, by the way, if you find yourself arguing after either of you had a couple of drinks...just stop. Pack it in. First, the part of your brain responsible for stopping you from saying stupid, hurtful shit? Yeah, that part was drinking too! And you're at greater risk of saying things that may be true but not at the best time. Second, who knows how much either of you will even remember the argument at a later date? Alcohol distorts memory, so there's no actual accurate memory of anything. It all vanishes as you sober up. So, congratulations, maybe you won; but it doesn't matter.

And last but not least, alcohol is a disinhibitor overall. The part of your brain that censors you and stops you from doing stupid shit? Yeah, that part is drunk, too. Alcohol doesn't make you an asshole. Alcohol makes it impossible to hide that you're an asshole.

It is like when someone makes a racist comment and then later tries to excuse it away, blaming it on the liquor. The liquor didn't make you prejudiced. You already were. It was lurking in the background. The booze stopped you from restraining yourself from saying it in front of the wrong people.

That means that even though you would normally inhibit yourself and follow established rules of engagement in an interaction, you would be less likely to do so while intoxicated. The only way to win that game is not to play. Drinking while angry, and arguing, sets the stage for everyone losing. Save it for another day.

MEN'S FRAGILITY

When I first got into this field, and even when I was growing up, if there was drama and there was a woman around, it was often an indicator that things would *not* get out of control. Women had a neutralizing effect. They were useful in helping men constrain some of their worst instincts. Nowadays, the differences between men and women are much less visible. Gang involvement for girls and women has been steadily on the rise for some time now. The gender-based stereotypes that girls internalize and boys externalize their emotions is just not as true as it used to be. Not only do girls get angry and potentially violent, but when they lash out, the damage is different. And it can be deeper, though less visible.

When two boys get into a fight, it's often skin on skin—very direct, very close—and the next day they're playing ball together. When two girls get into a fight, sometimes character assassination becomes their weapon of choice. A wolfpack mentality can take hold, and the "loser" often finds herself attacked on multiple levels. And with the proliferation of social media and the anonymity afforded the keyboard assassins among us, it can lead to a girl being emotionally destroyed in ways that were not possible before. So, the idea that girls are *always* the peacemakers is somewhat obsolete.

Our narrow and unforgiving beauty standards lead girls to be barraged with expectations that they're supposed to look particular ways—thin, feminine, young, and fertile, for example—leaving very little room for error. Unfortunately, appearance often drives value for women, especially as it impacts their ability to select a partner. They should accept that they will suck at math and science (complete bull-shit; every boy knows many girls who would wipe the floor with them in STEM classes) and that their salaries will be a meager percentage of their male counterparts (on average, about 15 percent less, depending upon the study).

So, how do girls respond to this constant sociocultural assault that whispers the message "You're not good enough" nearly from birth? And how do girls and women handle the low self-esteem that one would expect from unreasonable and unattainable demands on their physical appearance, to say nothing of how amenable, conciliatory, and selfless our society asks women to be? From my professional experience, everything starts with how girls play as very small children. We give girls dolls, and what do they do with them? They immediately go into role-playing. This is the mother, this is the father. This is the doctor, this is the patient, and so on. They create little harmonious families and communities in which there's a lot of collaboration and mutual dependence. They accelerate their understanding of relationships, and this sets the stage for them to deepen their social intelligence.

On the other hand, when we give dolls to boys, which are affectionately called "action figures," they smash them against each other and throw them at the wall. The boys engage in and really like horse-play, which is important by the way for male development, while girls learn about people. This is a very important distinction. And, by the way, the boys who also pay attention to social interactions have considerable success in relationships across the board, with boys and girls, and children and adults.

What happens to these socially sophisticated debutantes? They grow and thrive. They often do well in school and get teachers to give them extra help, favoring them, because they're pleasant and interactive in ways that help the teachers feel supportive. These little fellas may be more verbal and express themselves more easily, which just greases the wheels of their whole little lives. They know how to connect with people, which is a skill that goes a very long way in this world.

They manipulate people, which is non-pejorative; it just means they get people to do what they want. They're easy to be around. They're pleasant, social, empathetic, and warm, which makes giving them what they want *easier*. Manipulation doesn't have to be calculating or harmful; it's a requirement to success in life. These kids are persuasive, and having learned these skills early, they're at a tremendous advantage.

What happens to our growing little pre-testosterone males? Well, they have similar inadequacies as girls, but as society expects girls to have low self-esteem (and many master this assignment), boys are expected to know what to do from the beginning. They are not allowed to cry or say "I don't know what to do" or 'I need help." Boys, in an effort to match our masculine social expectations of them, work hard to save face and puff out their chests. Little Timmy says, "That's right! I fucked six girls." Timmy, you're eight years old. You don't even know where your dick is...

Basically, society beats the vulnerability out of them. Boys learn that vulnerability is weakness, and weakness is the kryptonite of masculinity. Girls, on the other hand, learn that asking for help is what's expected of them, and more often than not, help is available to them.

This fear of not knowing, being unsure, appearing vulnerable, or not being good enough sets the stage for male fragility that impacts how they deal with emotions—especially anger—throughout their lives. And what happens if they are not "man enough"? We throw gendered insults at them, as though being a girl is absolutely the worst thing a boy could be. "Don't be a pussy!" "Are you wearing a skirt?" 'You're crying like a girl.' Even in very small boys, being a boy is understood to mean strong, in charge, capable, or all-knowing. Being accused of being a girl is a grievous insult in kid world.

Somehow, the message gets through, even into the very young minds of our children: Men are the power brokers and women are weak. Vulnerability is a liability. Any sign of weakness means being of lower value. Having feelings, and being able to name and deal with their feelings, is the domain of soft people, girly people, and anger is a powerful sign of dominance.

As Betty White once pointed out, "Why do people say, 'Grow some balls'? Balls are weak and sensitive. If you really wanna get tough, grow a vagina. Those things really take a pounding!"

You wonder why we deify the stoic man? Well, if you need to fight a war, to storm the beaches of Normandy, you are not looking for a guy who is going to sit down and have an in-depth examination of their unconscious struggles and how they map into your sensitivities. You want a person who knows how to take care of business. Someone who will kill if necessary, who is tough, determined, undeterred, and dangerous. But guess what? It doesn't require testicles to be that way. There are some pretty badass women in the world. Regardless, this primarily remains the domain of the stoic man.

Society has many needs for these guys. However, there are also many reasons, rather obviously, why this is not the best way to be.

Stoicism does not tend to easily map onto compassion, reciprocity, and emotional intelligence. But it's also not mutually exclusive. Just like anger, as we've discussed, healthy men can adjust the flame of their stoicism, like they adjusted their anger, and vastly increase their emotional awareness. This means that the healthiest men can tend to their relationships. They can show compassion, take interest in others (and not just for their own gain), and be well-rounded humans, not just the stoic machines we often teach boys to be.

Yet, what is most missing from all of this is permission. Boys are rarely given permission to be human, to not know, to be confused or scared or angry. Well, maybe that is the exception. Boys and men get angry. We almost come to expect it, but the *what* is not nearly as important as the *why* or the *how*.

People are insecure. Men are people. Do the math. It simply isn't the case that jealousy is only seen in women. Men get worried that they'll lose what they have. Terrified that they may be betrayed or, even worse, alone. So, unwilling to explore its origins and how to accept and fix these issues, some men become controlling. Ironically, the more they try to control others, the more they drive people away. The thing they are most afraid of they make happen, in a tragic self-fulfilling prophecy.

Insecurity feels weak and vulnerable. Fortunately, we have some anger in our back pocket, and men are supposed to wield it by acting like a raging asshole. But hey, it certainly feels more powerful than the alternative, doesn't it? Yet, the chronically angry person will often wind up alone...unless they do something about it. Understanding anger serves to validate its origins (in this case for insecure men) and gives us all the power to choose a different path.

To take this one step further, there has been a fair amount of discussion about how toxic masculinity contributes to sexual violence. Toxic (or hostile) masculinity does not presume anything about all men, or about masculinity in general. It's a subset of masculinity that rests on several principles that I would contend all stem from insecurity.

The hallmarks are based upon these expectations: men should be tough, masculine, and powerful. These are not terribly well defined, but as Joe Ehrmann, former Baltimore Colt and now counselor/lecturer pointed out in his TED Talk "Be A Man," boys are socialized to believe that their value is based upon their forty time, the size of their wallet, and the number of girls they've slept with. When he interviewed men on their deathbeds, not a single one of them was talking about those things. They were talking about two things that make a human a man: their legacy, meaning the mark they are leaving on the world, and the quality of their relationships.

When boys are taught this, they can grow into men who can run the gamut from the stoic hero in a time of need to the sensitive, thoughtful, family man who takes care of the people around him. We need more men at the table teaching boys this, and getting a handle on our fucking anger is the first step.

But since we don't actively teach this, we have a lot of confused, emotionally stifled, angry men walking around and smoldering in our midst. And further, because anger has so much shame attached to it, what do you get when you ask a man why he's so angry? His response, all too often, is, "I'm not FUCKING ANGRY!!!"

Yeah, you are, and it's okay. What you *do* with that anger is what counts.

QUOTES ON ANGER

People have been thinking about, talking about, and writing about anger for a long, long time, because it's been part of humanity for as long as people have been here. Anger isn't news, but using it to adjust the flame and get what you want from life is. We will conclude with some of my favorite quotes, many of which I learned through a long career of examining anger in people.

* * *

"Football is about controlling that anger, harnessing that aggression into a team effort to achieve perfection!"

—Actor Denzel Washington as Coach Herman Boone
in *Remember the Titans*

"I can't afford the luxury of anger. Anger can make me vulnerable. It can destroy my reason, and reason is the only advantage I have over them."

—Actor Vincent Price as Dr. Robert Morgan
in *The Last Man on Earth* (1964)

"Anybody can become angry—that is easy, but to be angry with the right person and to the right degree and at the right time and for the right purpose, and in the right way—that is not within everybody's power and is not easy."

—Ancient Greek philosopher Aristotle

"You got anger. That's good. You're gonna need it, son. You got aggression. That's even better. You're gonna need that, too, but any two-year-old child can throw a fit."

—Actor Denzel Washington as Coach Herman Boone
in *Remember the Titans*

"That's my secret, Captain. I'm always angry."

—Actor Mark Ruffalo as Bruce Banner/Hulk
in *The Avengers* (2012)

"Anger is an acid that can do more harm to the vessel in which it is stored than to anything on which it is poured."

—Writer Mark Twain

"When angry, count to ten before you speak. If very angry, count to one hundred."

—Founding Father Thomas Jefferson

"Love implies anger. The man who is angered by nothing cares about nothing."

—Author Edward Abbey

"I can feel your anger. It gives you focus, makes you stronger."

—Actor Ian McDiarmid as Emperor Palpatine/Darth Sidious
in *Star Wars: Episode III—Revenge of the Sith*

"Speak when you are angry—and you'll make the best speech you'll ever regret."

—Educator Laurence J. Peter

"In times of great stress or adversity, it's always best to keep busy, to plow your anger and your energy into something positive."

—Automobile executive Lee Iacocca

"There's always a place for the angry young man
With his fist in the air and his head in the sand.
He's never been able to learn from mistakes
He can't understand why his heart always breaks."

—Singer/songwriter Billy Joel

"I had such anger back then. When you're young a lot of people do. Everybody does. You're pissed—and you're not sure why—because you want to express something, but you don't know what it is. She [his acting teacher] kept telling me to go ahead, but I never wanted to. I think she told a partner to do something to me and he did it, and I destroyed the place—and then at the end of it—I remember my hands were bleeding a little bit—and she goes, 'See, everybody's fine. Nobody's hurt. This is what you have to do. This is what people pay for. If you don't want to do it, get off—these are the things you need to express and be able to control.'"

—Actor James Gandolfini

"I sense great fear in you, Skywalker. You have hate. You have anger. But you don't use them."

—Actor Christopher Lee as Count Dooku/Darth Tyranus
in *Star Wars: Episode III—Revenge of the Sith*

"The greatest remedy for anger is delay."

—Ancient Roman philosopher Lucius Annaeus Seneca

"Expressing anger appropriately is essential to mental health. Repressing it is not."

—American psychiatrist Aaron T. Beck

"He who angers you, conquers you."

—Nineteenth-century self-taught Australian
bush nurse Elizabeth Kenny

"Holding onto anger is like drinking poison and expecting the other person to die."

—Fifth-century religious teacher Buddha

"Temper's the one thing you can't get rid of by losing it."

—Actor Jack Nicholson as Dr. Buddy Rydell
in *Anger Management*

"Football is a violent sport, and if you don't kind of go to that dark place to be violent and be physical, you're not going to last very long."

—Professional football player George Kittle

"Anger is like a check-engine light—it doesn't tell you what's broken, just that you need to look under the hood."

—American academic Brad Bushman

"Uncontrolled rage is a primitive defense against vulnerability."

—American Researcher, teacher, and psychiatrist Judith Herman

"Fear is the path to the dark side. Fear leads to anger. Anger leads to hate. Hate leads to suffering."

—Jedi Master Yoda (who was wrong, by the way...)

"If you're ever in a situation where you need to seek revenge, do it in cold blood, not hot blood. With hot blood, you make mistakes."

—Lloyd Abrams, Father, husband, and man of uncommon decency

And finally, a few of my own:

"You want to talk about being tough? The toughest guy in prison never fights. He doesn't have to. Really being tough is when you cannot be provoked."

—Mitch Abrams

"Rage is not an emotion to be extinguished—it's one to be understood before it explodes."

—Mitch Abrams

"There's only a one-letter difference between anger and danger. That 'D' stands for discipline. Without discipline, that anger can become very dangerous."

—Mitch Abrams

ACKNOWLEDGMENTS

To my wife, Christy, the glue to my world. Your strength, patience, and unwavering belief in me made this book possible. You hold everything together, even when I come unglued. I love you more than words can express. TMLB

To Lea Nicole, you've always found a way to rise, no matter the odds. I look forward to all of the great things that your resilience and brilliance bring you.

To Aviva Elle, thank you for teaching me what it truly means to be unapologetically yourself. Your courage to live boldly and authentically inspires me every day. I don't know how you let everything roll off your back, but it is impressive. I have no doubt you will go get what you want.

To Mason Alexander, our diamond. Strong, unbreakable, and shining bright. You're made of tough stuff, kid, and I couldn't be prouder. Never stop laughing! You are infectious.

And most importantly, to Logan Benjamin, my first and best effort at raising a boy into a man. An absolutely better version of me. One who knows it's okay to be sensitive, angry, hilarious, and affectionate. I love the fact that life gets easy when you and I are together. It has been a privilege to watch you grow into the man you are becoming. I love you, son!

To my parents, Lloyd and Barbara Abrams. Though I grew up money poor, I was rich in the only currency that truly matters: love, support, and unwavering belief. You reminded me constantly that I was valuable, even when the world tried to convince me otherwise. No matter how hard I fell out there, I always had a safe space to land, a home that gave me the strength to get back up and go on the attack. I stand on your shoulders every day, carrying your lessons, your love, and your resilience into everything I do. I miss you both terribly. Thank you for giving me the kind of wealth that never runs out.

To my sister, Alicia. My first peer and the first person I argued with. Losing you at twenty years old shattered our family. I often think about how our lives would have been. I miss you dearly.

This book is for all of you. You've shaped me, fueled me, and reminded me why this work matters. I'm not fucking angry—I'm full of love for all of you. Don't ever forget it!

ABOUT THE AUTHOR

Dr. Mitch Abrams is a sport, clinical, and forensic psychologist, licensed in NY and NJ, and CEO of Learned Excellence for Athletes and Abrams Psychological Services, which has offices in New Jersey but has consulted nationally for over 25 years. He is THE nation's expert on anger in sports, as well as having expertise in sexual and domestic violence, in addition to trauma. He has developed comprehensive prevention programs, including the Abrams Model of Sexual Violence Prevention, which integrates forensic concepts in sport psychology approaches. As a pioneer, he also developed Entourage Training, a system that takes a member of the athlete's peer group and trains them in conflict resolution, gang identification, social media training, prediction of consequences, and directs them towards self-defense and weapons training as needed. Not only has he developed these innovations, Dr. Abrams has also trained sport psychologists, parents, sports organizations, and coaches about these issues.

Having worked inside the New Jersey State Prison system since 2000, he has twenty-five years of correctional experience and is the Chief Psychologist for University Correctional Health Care, Rutgers University's service delivery arm which provides medical, dental, and mental health services for the New Jersey Department of Corrections.

He is also on faculty at Rutgers Robert Wood Johnson Medical School and has been adjunct faculty at Brooklyn College, Fairleigh Dickinson University, and Long Island University – Post Campus.

In addition to *I'm Not F*cking Angry!, Dr. Abrams wrote *Anger Management in Sport – Understanding and Controlling Violence in Athletes* in 2010. He has also written journal articles and book chapters focusing on anger, violence, and trauma in sport populations.

Dr. Abrams is a Fellow of both Division 47 of the American Psychological Association, The Society for Sport, Exercise & Performance Psychology, and the Association of Applied Sport Psychology, where he founded and co-chairs the Anger & Violence in Sport Special Interest Group.

His expertise has led to consulting beyond sport and forensic audiences, as he has spoken at national conferences, consulted with CEOs and other C-Suite executives, and has frequently been called upon to provide insight into different areas of deviant behavior in the media.

Undeniably, Dr. Abrams is a kid from the streets. He was raised in Starrett City, an area of Brooklyn, New York, that molded much of his world view. He received his Bachelor of Science from Brooklyn College and earned his Master of Science in Applied Psychology and his Doctorate of Psychology (Psy.D.) in Clinical Psychology from C.W. Post/Long Island University.

For more information or to contact the author, visit:
DrMitchAbrams.com

www.ingramcontent.com/pod-product-compliance
Lightning Source LLC
Chambersburg PA
CBHW071743120626
46550CB00002B/636